George Santayana's America

George Santayana's America

ESSAYS ON LITERATURE AND CULTURE

*Collected and with an
Introduction by
James Ballowe*

UNIVERSITY OF ILLINOIS PRESS, URBANA · CHICAGO · LONDON, 1967

This soil is propitious to every seed, and tares must needs grow in it; but why should it not also breed clear thinking, honest judgment, and rational happiness?

Santayana, Preface, *Character and Opinion in the United States*

A Note on the Text

These essays by George Santayana are here collected for the first time. They reveal his opinions on American literature and culture from 1886, the year in which he graduated from Harvard, to 1922, two years after he published *Character and Opinion in the United States*. The reader interested in Santayana's views on America should find these essays to be complementary to Santayana's works on America which have previously appeared in book form. These latter works are discussed in Part II of my Introduction, thus providing a survey of Santayana's major criticism of American life and letters. My notes to each section are designed to emphasize the consistency of his criticism and to suggest the relation of these selections to the body of his critical works on America.

The idea for this collection was given to me by Professor Sherman Paul, who also introduced me to Santayana when he was my graduate adviser at the University of Illinois. His helpful guidance and continued encouragement have been largely responsible for the successful completion of this book. I am also indebted to the Bradley University Faculty Research Committee for funds to work on this project. For help in obtaining materials, I want to thank Miss Eva Faye Benton of the English Library at the University of Illinois and Mrs. Anna Johnson and Mrs. Elizabeth Bryan of the Bradley University Library.

For permissions to use the essays in this book, I am indebted to Mr. Daniel Cory, Santayana's literary executor, for use of "The Optimism of Ralph Waldo Emerson" and for his approval of the project; to the *Boston Latin School Register for* "Glimpses of Old Boston"; and to the *Oberlin Alumni Magazine* for "Tradition and Practice." A portion of Part II of my Introduction is taken from my article "*The Last Puritan* and the Failure in American Culture," *American Quarterly*, XVIII (Summer, 1966), and is used here with permission of the editors. The remaining essays and the illustration are in the public domain, but I have acknowledged their sources at the beginning of each essay.

The editions I used for the quotations from Santayana's works in my Introduction are as follows:

Charles Scribner's Sons, New York: *Dominations and Powers* (1951); *The Letters of George Santayana*, ed. Daniel Cory (1955); *Persons and Places*, vols. I, II, III (1944, 1945, 1953); and *The Works of George Santayana*, Triton Edition, 15 vols. (1936–40) for *Character and Opinion in the United States, Interpretations of Poetry and Religion, The Life of Reason*, vol. I: *Reason in Common Sense*, and *Winds of Doctrine*.

George Braziller, Inc., New York: *The Idler and His Works*, ed. Daniel Cory (1957).

Northwestern University Press, Evanston, Ill.: "Apologia pro Menta Sua" and "A General Confession," in *The Library of Living Philosophers*, ed. Paul Arthur Schilpp, vol. II: *The Philosophy of George Santayana* (1940).

Contents

Introduction

Part III

Introduction

BIOGRAPHY AND CRITICISM

I

The facts of George Santayana's life are well known. Outlined briefly they show him in various parts of the western world living the life of the disinterested observer. He was born to Spanish parents in Madrid on December 16, 1863. But his mother left Spain in 1869 to fulfill a pledge to her first husband, the Bostonian Robert Sturgis (who died in 1857), to bring up their children in New England. After remaining in Avila, Spain, for three years with his father, Santayana joined his Sturgis half-brother and two half-sisters in Boston in 1872. During the next fourteen years he attended kindergarten, public grammar school, the Boston Latin School, and Harvard College. After his first year at Harvard, in 1883, he began a yearly pilgrimage to Avila, first to visit his father and later his half-sister Susana. Her death in 1930 left him without a close personal attachment in Avila, although he continued to think of it as his home. His European trips grew more frequent and prolonged. He was given a two-year graduate fellowship in Germany (1886–88) and had two sabbatical leaves (1896–97 and 1905–07) from Harvard, where he began teaching philosophy in 1889. Having interrupted his American sojourn with "thirty-eight fussy voyages" abroad, he left Harvard abruptly and for good in 1912. He lived in Spain, England, and

Paris until World War I; then he was marooned at Oxford from
1914 to 1919. Increasingly after the war he made his home in
Rome, spending summers in Paris and on the Riviera. Finally, at
the age of seventy-seven, he became a permanent resident of the
Blue Sisters' Nursing Home near the Santo Stefano Rotondo in
Rome. He thought and worked steadily but with increasing physical difficulty until his death on September 26, 1952.

Santayana's southern European ancestry, his continual gravitation to Europe during his forty-year residence in America, and
his final self-exile to the Old World seem to support the opinion
that his relationship with America was tenuous. On the surface a
pre-birth pledge, the necessity of education, and a relatively
innocuous profession are all that held him to America. In his
autobiography *Persons and Places,* III (1953), he writes that
during his active life he had never felt comfortable in any country. He was an inveterate traveler on a private odyssey. Although
his residence was mainly in the North, he had never been com-
pletely at rest there. Not until he was faced with old age did he
finally arrive at a "predestined resting place" where he could be
ubiquitous without leaving his "fated centre of gravity and equi-
librium." This was Rome, which possessed the intrinsic vitality of
"balance and wisdom that comes from long perspectives and
broad foundations." Twenty-eight years after leaving America
Santayana wrote in his "Apologia pro Menta Sua" that with
freedom of choice he would not have sought education in America, nor would he have taught philosophy there or anywhere else.
His account of his Americanism shows how meager his physical
attachment to America actually was: "Harvard College, a part of
Boston, an occasional glimpse of New York made up my America. . . . I have no American or English blood; I was not born in
the United States; I have never become an American citizen; as
soon as I was my own master I spent every free winter and
almost every summer in Europe; I never married or kept house or
expected to end my days in America."

A few years later in *Persons and Places,* I (1944), Santayana
was to reflect on his American residence by comparing it with
what might have been had he remained in Spain. Although his
education in Boston had been steadier and his friendships more
regular and calmer than they would have been in Spain, he was
morally disinherited and felt an "emotional and intellectual chill,"
resulting from a "pettiness and practicality of outlook" in

America. He presumed that he would not have been confronted with such a feeling in a Spanish environment with its "complex passions and intrigues." Although his Spanish education probably would have lacked the same degree of solidity and thoroughness as did his New England education, he believed that the Spanish "wind of politics and of poetry" would have swelled the bits of learning and sublimated them with an honor unavailable in American schools. Even so, he concluded that a Spanish education would have given him entirely different perspectives, and he would not have been the man that he became. For this reason, Santayana felt that his father's decision to leave him at the Beacon Street residence of his mother was, in the last analysis, all for his own good. He could only conclude, as he did in the preface to *Character and Opinion in the United States* (1920), that America and American philosophy had aided in clearing and settling his mind.

What contributed to molding his identity were not those things which are nostalgically recalled by a man reflecting on the important influences of his youth. Great portions of his American experience were viewed by him as somnambulistic. He knew *"persons* and *places,"* but not himself. Two-thirds of his Latin School days, he relates, were spent as "if I hadn't existed, or only as a mechanical sensorium and active apparatus, doing its work under my name." This statement tends to indicate the surface reaction the philosopher and critic had to experiences which might have been invaluable to his contemporaries in America.

Yet his lack of sympathy for his American environment was compensated for by a cultivated philosophical detachment and a natural capacity to see the humor of his situation. When he began to gain public recognition—as when at sixteen he received the school poetry prize for a long Spenserian poem describing the superiority of Night over Day—he felt that his childhood shyness and love of solitude took on a higher form. His mature outlook allowed him to substitute for his earlier timidity a rebelliousness "against being roped in and made to play some vulgar trick in a circus." His choice of a solitary life was freely made: he no longer feared the world but claimed his liberty and *Lebensraum* beyond it. It became possible for him to form an objectively impartial attitude toward all experience. As he grew older, he came to feel sorrow rather than rage of spirit when he recognized a "lapse of natural perfection" in a world which could not meet the stand-

ards Nature had set for it. But this discontent was mitigated
throughout his life by his gift of laughter, which helped him "to
perceive those defects and to put up with them." In 1887, he
wrote from Berlin to his friend Henry Ward Abbot that he had
all along cultivated the "point of view of the easy chair," or "the
point of view of the grave." "A man in his grave is not only
apathetic," he wrote, "but also invulnerable," able to recognize
"the universal joke" without having to risk its consequences. In
an epicurean mood he maintained that "the idea of demanding
that things should be worth doing is a human impertinence."
Still, he concluded that this point of view is not simple to attain:
"It is not gained except by renunciation. Pleasure must first cease
to attract and pain to repel. . . . I beg of you, let us remember
that the joke of things is one at our expense. It is very funny, but
it is exceedingly unpleasant."

His philosophical detachment and his ability to see his environment ironically are the central elements in Santayana's cultural criticism of America. When he discovered that he had to
live for a long time in an atmosphere hostile to his pursuits, his
humor sustained him. Echoes in his autobiography indicate his
intellectual detachment: he remained at the Latin School, as he
remained at Harvard for over twenty-five years, "a stranger at
heart." As a student at Harvard he "never had a real friend who
was a professor." As a teacher there he confirmed himself in the
belief that "the intellectual world of [his] time alienated [him]
intellectually." In President Eliot's Harvard he found that the
intellectual pursuits suffered because professors were "too much
overworked, too poor, too much tied up in their modest homes.
Nor had they had, like old-fashioned English dons, a common
education, and written Latin hexameters and pentameters."
There was no literary fashion. Save perhaps for Professor C. H.
Toy, whose wife entertained Santayana at teas, and William
James and Charles Eliot Norton, with whom he was on good
terms, the entire faculty struck him as "an anonymous concourse
of coral insects, each secreting one cell, and leaving that fossil
legacy to enlarge the earth."[1]

---

[1] Santayana also admired Barrett Wendell, whose undergraduate and
teaching years at Harvard nearly paralleled his own. But they remained at a
distance from one another, although Santayana thought they "were on the

From the outset Santayana was at odds with President Eliot, who never actively supported him for his first Harvard appointment nor for a long overdue promotion. For Eliot "education meant preparation for professional life. College, and all that occupied the time and mind of the College, and seemed to the College an end in itself, seemed to President Eliot only a means. The end was service in the world of business."[2] The antihumanist Eliot once suggested to Santayana that he should teach the facts, not convey ideas. But for Santayana, who felt that the "history of philosophy is the only philosophy that should be taught in a university," the systems he saw being expounded at Harvard at the expense of the students were the products of "individuals eager to found sects." System-making was always anathema to him. Even after he had himself devised a philosophical system, he meant it "to be only a contribution to the humanities, the expression of a reflective, selective, and free mind." Yet as a scholar Santayana gave in to the Harvard emphasis on a specialty. His first course on aesthetics resulted in *The Sense of Beauty* (1896); a course in the philosophy of history yielded *The Life of Reason* (1905–06). But these courses were not aimed at forcing a system on anyone. The goals of his college were foreign to him and it was his own aesthetic leanings which set him constitutionally at odds with the Harvard administration and thus with the cultural center of his time and place.[3]

---

same side of the barricade." Wendell seemed less prepared to display his sympathies in the face of the administration. (For Wendell's eccentricities see William Lyon Phelps, *Autobiography with Letters* [New York, Oxford University Press, 1939].)

[2] In "The Academic Environment," in *Character and Opinion in the United States,* Santayana characterized Eliot as being entirely concerned about quantity rather than quality. Santayana's contemporary John Jay Chapman also portrayed Eliot as a man who dedicated his life to the ideal that quantity comes before quality in a civilization. Chapman's essay on Eliot reveals that Eliot destroyed two things at Harvard and, consequently, in American higher education: the pupil-teacher relationship and the vitality of individual minds. (See "President Eliot," in *The Selected Writings of John Jay Chapman,* ed. Jacques Barzun [New York, Farrar, Straus and Cudahy, Inc., 1957].)

[3] Having attained the Walker Fellowship for two years of graduate work in Germany, Santayana at first indulged in scholarship which interested him. When he was reprimanded by William James for his lack of progress toward the degree, Santayana replied in words which characterize his distance from the methodology of Harvard: "it is very doubtful that I should ever get a

In summarizing his professional career at Harvard in *Persons
and Places,* II (1945), Santayana lists the "sins" he had commit-
ted which gained him disfavor during his twenty-three-year tenure and which indicated that he was not in the mainstream of
American progress: he had not become a specialist; he had
written "pessimistic, old-fashioned verses"; he was "indiscernibly
a Catholic or atheist"; he had attacked Robert Browning,
"prophet of the half-educated and unbelieving"; he had avoided
administrative duties; he had kept to "the society of undergraduates and old ladies"; he had spent his holidays abroad; and he
had been a witness in the much-publicized divorce trial of Lord
Russell, his close friend and the brother of Bertrand Russell.

But also in a literary sense Santayana's temperament was not
coincident with that of his environment. He once remarked that
"English, and the whole Anglo-Saxon tradition in literature and
philosophy, have always been a medium to me rather than a
source. My natural affinities were elsewhere." His promising
poetic career was cut short because that medium emphasized the
difference between his temperament and that of others at home
in the environment. The language, he wrote, "was only a symbol
for the much more hopelessly foreign quality of the English sort
of imagination, and the northern respect for the inner man instead of the southern respect for the great world, for fate, for
history, for matter." Poetry demands an attitude commensurate
with its terms of expression; Santayana's attitude evolved from a
life of reason and could not emotionally wed the sense and the
sound of the North.

Yet had Santayana's criticism of Anglo-Saxon America been
based solely on the fact that the English imagination was foreign
to his own way of thinking, he would have been able to offer only
a partial and suspect criticism. There were closer and more
elemental ties than those of education and vocation. In the first
place, Santayana could trace his roots in America back two
generations. His maternal grandfather José Borrás, a political and

---

professorship anyway, and I hardly care to sacrifice my tastes to that bare
possibility . . . what I shall write will certainly not smack so much of a
professorship as if it were on the normal jerk of the kneepan." (See the
letter quoted in Ralph Barton Perry, *The Thought and Character of William
James* [Boston, Atlantic–Little, Brown and Co., 1935], vol. I.)

religious exile from Spain, had moved from Glasgow to Virginia, where he found the Jeffersonian democracy of Winchester agreeable to his deistic-democratic idealism. This incongruity of place made it necessary for Santayana's mother to spend her first years in the United States. After her father was reconciled with the Spanish government, he returned to Spain as an American consul. Later he was sent by Spain to the Philippines as a government representative. But Santayana points out that Josefina Borrás never forgot the lessons of her early residence in America. She had learned from her father and his eighteenth-century American idealism not only "the eternal truths" of the Enlightenment, which Pope's *Essay on Man* contains "in crisp epigrams," but also the social lesson that "refinement . . . excluded any real vices." She was prepared early for an entry into the gentility of Boston which later was made possible by her marriage to George Sturgis, a United States official in Manila. Upon Sturgis' death, she moved with her three children to a socially insular and complacently materialistic Boston. There she believed she could find the refinement she had missed. Although Santayana felt that her Boston relationships, "always friendly and theoretically cordial," were never close, they were close enough that the Sturgises provided her with an annual fund for her family, a fund which Santayana benefited from when he came to America. In later years his mother lived in Roxbury, having moved from her more fashionable home on Beacon Street; her life was that of a recluse, and her family spoke Spanish. She was so withdrawn that although Santayana visited her on Sundays throughout the years at Harvard, few of his friends knew that his family was living close by.[4] Even though he seems never to have been close to his mother, her death in 1912 (the year he left Harvard) was a major factor in his decision not to return to the United States.

To Santayana his grandfather, mother, and even his own father

---

[4] What Santayana writes of his mother's life in Boston is in a measure true of his own. He felt that she "resented the tendency, meant for kindness, to assimilate and absorb her, and she emphasized her separateness in self-defense, as I had to do afterwards in personal and intellectual matters. Boston was a nice place with very nice people in it; but it was an excellent point of vantage from which to start out, if you belonged there, rather than a desirable point to arrive at if you were born in some other place. It was a moral and intellectual nursery, always busy applying first principles to trifles."

were a personal link with pre–Civil War Boston, which impressed him because it possessed an identifiable culture. Only
remnants of this culture could be found in his own time. His
father, also an official in the Philippines, was a friend of the
Sturgises before George's death. An inveterate traveler like his
son, he sailed to Boston with the Sturgises in 1856, on his way to
Spain. After this visit Agustín Santayana had written enthusiastically of "the lovely scene in some genteel suburb of Boston"
which seemed "the perfection of human existence, at last realized
on earth." The younger Santayana in turn wrote pensively of the
enlightened Boston of the 1850's: "There were gentle lights burning in some of those houses, with no exaggeration of their bril-
liance: Ticknors, Parkmans, Longfellows and Lowells with their
various modest and mature minds. I came too late to gather
much of that quiet spirit of colonial culture, that felt itself to be
secondary and a bit remote from its sources, and yet was proud
of its remoteness, which gave it the privilege of being universal
and just." In Santayana's time this spirit lingered in Charles Eliot
Norton, "saddened," however, "by the sense of being a survival."
The giants of the mid-century were mere shadows by the time
Santayana came to America. He recalls having only fleeting
glimpses of the literary hierarchy. He knew Lowell, had shaken
hands with Longfellow, and, while still a resident of Beacon
Street, was a neighbor of Dr. Holmes. But he never saw Emerson,
of whom he was to write at length in later years.

In Santayana's youth New England retained two vestiges of
puritan gentility: the church and cultivated Boston society. Santayana went regularly with his sister Susana to Mass. But often—upon the encouragement of his mother—he attended Unitarian services on the same day. He found religion to be the chief
source of familial and moral discord. He was forced to witness a
sustained conflict between deism and Catholicism. As a result of
the insight he gained from this conflict and from historical and
psychological study, he came to view religion as an invention of
the mind, "all conceived and worked out inwardly, imaginatively,
for moral reasons." Thus he was confirmed early in agnosticism,
which gave him freedom of movement in predominantly non-
Catholic Boston society. One of the great disappointments of
Santayana's life was the fact that Susana had allowed her Catholicism to become a source of fanaticism in a very conventional and

evidently American fashion. Lacking the capacity for specula-
tion, she had turned religion into "a problem and a torment"
instead of finding in it a "peace and a secret symbolic life."

Santayana saw at first hand the religiosity of conservative
Boston Unitarianism. He writes, "I had heard many Unitarian
sermons (being taken to hear them lest I should become too
Catholic), and had been interested in them so far as they were
rationalistic and informative, or even amusingly irreligious, as I
often thought them to be; but neither in those discourses nor in
Harvard philosophy was it easy for me to understand the Protestant combination of earnestness with waywardness. I was used to
see water flowing from the fountains, architectural and above
ground: it puzzled me to see it drawn painfully in bucketfuls
from the subjective well, muddied, and half spilt over." Lacking
theological justification, these puritans seemed ridiculous to him
as they flocked together on Sundays. Socially self-conscious, they
went to hear journalistic sermons which were "calculated to
confirm the conviction already in them that their bourgeois
virtues were quite sufficient and that perhaps in time poor backward races and nations might be led to acquire them." They
assumed an air of higher snobbery, forcing the enlightenment
with which they were blessed upon the unchosen ones.

Although he proclaimed of himself that he had never been
"what is called a practicing Catholic," he nevertheless saw things
from a Catholic viewpoint—a perspective which he had attained
naturally as a result of "sympathy and allegiance, not of philosophy." Yet he never seriously considered religion as dogma. He
"indulged in it, but only north-northwest." His *afición* for Catholicism was aesthetic rather than philosophical. From the time of
his early interest in the architecture of churches to his later
identification of the poetic and religious in *Interpretations of
Poetry and Religion* (1900), Santayana insisted that religion
was simply another subject matter on which his fancy could
work. Like architecture, religion provided him "with new materials for . . . dreams, and other terms in which to express [his]
secret aspiration." He viewed religious institutions as means by
which man may be transported: "The end is to escape to another
world, to live freely for awhile in a medium made by us and fit
for us to live in."

From his religious experiences Santayana formed his attitudes toward Protestant America. His religious criticism was carried on without benefit of having implicit faith in any systematic religion. To the youthful Santayana, as to many of his contemporaries, religion had produced an irreconcilable dilemma. In "A General Confession" (1930), looking back to his youth, he wrote that "if religion was false everything was worthless, and almost everything, if religion was true." He recognized that this youthful pessimism was "hardly more foolish than [that of] so many amateur mediaevalists and religious aesthetes of my generation," and he "saw the same alternative between Catholicism and complete disillusion"; then he shows his affinity for Spinoza by concluding, "I was never afraid of disillusion, and I have chosen it." His mature conclusion is not far from his earlier, less philosophically based attitude: he learned to view the "so-called real world" as a product of the imagination, and religion as providing a system of faith extending beyond the vulgar one. He wrote that religion expresses "destiny in moral dimensions, in obviously mythical and poetical images. . . . Religions are the great fairy-tales of the conscience."

Santayana was as much an anomaly in Boston society as he was in a Unitarian congregation. But all of his life he yearned for intellectual and sophisticated companionship, which in Boston was to be found only among the rich. He knew that Bostonians prized his participation in their cultural world for the obvious reason that with his foreign background he added something exotic to it, and for the more subtle reason that he could often comment on their habits with an impunity that they themselves did not possess. Santayana found that to many Bostonians he "was such a relief!" He was not a native, or a visiting foreigner, or a member of an eccentric profession (Harvard professors were commonplace in Boston society). But in his peculiar relationship to this society he was able to skirmish "on the borders of the polite world." This was largely a society of ladies. It was led by Mrs. John L. "Jack" Gardner and Mrs. Sarah Wyman Whitman. Although these women and their entourage seem to exemplify the final decay of the aestheticism of the nineteenth century, Santayana admired both for being passionately devoted to the arts and for being certain of their aims. Even if he himself was motivated by a somewhat reserved yearning for social position that could make him comfortable and satisfy his epicurean tastes, he found in this make-believe culture one other experience which he could glean while he was passing his time at Harvard.

Santayana had enough personal charm and talent to be asked to participate also in the society of his classmates at the Latin School and at Harvard. Protesting to an early commentator on his life who said that he had lived an isolated life in America, Santayana enumerated those extracurricular events in which he had taken part: he was lieutenant colonel of the Boston School Regiment; he acted in the Institute and Hasty Pudding plays at Harvard, dressed as a leading lady and a ballet dancer; he was a devoted spectator of football; and he had many young undergraduate friends when he was a Harvard instructor. At Harvard, too, Santayana counted the O.K. and *The Harvard Monthly* (of which he was an original editor) as the two most important literary groups to which he belonged. The nucleus for both was the undergraduate *Lampoon* staff, on which Santayana had served as cartoonist. But even with all of these evidences of participation, Santayana was accused by A. B. Houghton, the founder of the *Monthly* (later ambassador at Berlin and London), of swimming against the dominant contemporary current. On the other hand, Santayana felt that Houghton and others who were accustomed to "rush down the very middle of the rapids and rejoice in their speed" criticized themselves by such accusations. For his part he "merely stood on the bank or paddled about in the quiet backwater . . . [and] observed that the torrent was carrying down more or less wreckage." Santayana was willing to participate in and observe American life. But his activity was carried on with discretion, and he could never enter into anything as if it were all that mattered. America was like a team in a football match; it had a defined goal to which it was vigorously heading by sheer physical force and practical experimentation. Santayana preferred to be a sympathetic spectator, a sophisticate in the midst of the barbarians who were engaged in the struggle for success.

Not all of Santayana's American associations were accidental, reserved, or made with ulterior motives. If the breadth of American institutions was to be judged by their New England prototypes, the depth of the society was to be plumbed in the youth of New England. Individual American acquaintances were the most

rewarding for Santayana. His friendships—and many were transitory—were sublimated by years of reflection so that they were
eventually conceived by him as symbolic of the American psyche.
The most significant of his few friends during Boston Latin days
was his first and perhaps his "fundamental model" for the hero of
his novel *The Last Puritan* (1935). This was Edward Bayley,
destined to be a comrade for only a year. But the transitoriness of
the friendship apparently was enough to awaken in Santayana's
imagination during the next sixty years a complete picture of a
strictly puritan, inward religion which produced—as it did in his
hero Oliver Alden—both charity and hospitality of mind. The
transposition of Bayley into Oliver was an act of the imagination
in which Santayana read ideals of his own into his friend. He
assumed Bayley was the truly charitable puritan, absolutely loyal
to his own tradition but possessing an "affection for what he
excluded from his own sphere." Also like Oliver he was an athlete
and a leader; he was colonel of the public school regiment in
which Santayana served. Santayana imagined Bayley's spiritual
heritage to be that of Milton and of the young Emerson (the
"Puritan Goethe" who wrote *Nature*, rather than the later Emerson who, Santayana believed, had "slipped into transcendentalism and moralism and complacency in mediocrity"). He was a
"dumb inglorious Milton who was not a prig, an Emerson with
warm blood, who was not proud or oracular or cosmographical,
and never thought himself the center of the universe." Even
though Bayley was not all this when Santayana knew him (and
no doubt never became so), his demeanor promised much that
was realized in Santayana's later companions who had similar
training and background.

Not until he was a Harvard undergraduate did Santayana
begin to discover that many of these New England descendants
of America's puritan patriarchs were following a disastrous
course. They were unable or unwilling to extricate themselves
from the conservative security of their fathers and face anew the
problems of their own age. They had the spirit of an admirable
epoch, but it was incompatible with the new era. This was first
made clear to Santayana by his Sturgis family relations. He came
to read in this family the disintegration of the Great Merchants of
the mid-nineteenth century. For half a lifetime he "had the
melancholy pleasure of watching them in their early glory and in

their gradual obscuration, dispersion and decline." This decline was developed by Santayana into a leitmotif: "The first great, slow, tremendous variation upon it was made by the splendid Russell Sturgis himself. Of his great days," Santayana writes, "I have seen many traces, all his children's households were at first prosperous, fresh, luxurious, recognizable copies of the parental grandeur; but the reflection paled, as the sun itself descended."

The theme was played in full by the Sturgis family. But at Harvard Santayana encountered its numerous variations. As the traditional center of culture for New England, Harvard was the focal point for the scions of the Great Merchant families. The eleven years as student, instructor, and proctor that he lived in the Harvard Yard were compensation enough for the unkindness of fortune which had placed him in a time and place conflicting with his nature. There Santayana could observe closely, as friends and students, a number of these young men. The grandsons of Emerson and John Forbes (a wealthy Cape Cod merchant), of Russell Sturgis, and of a Civil War general by the name of Barlow symbolized the dissolution of the Great Merchant economy caused by its incapacity to continue for more than three generations. This incapacity, Santayana wrote, was inherent in the system itself: "Either their fortune was inadequate, or their virtue was inadequate, or their health and stamina were inadequate. Gently, or sadly, or cynically, they had to bow themselves off the stage. . . . These grandsons, these essential descendants, couldn't merge [into "the vast American vortex"]." His close friends Cameron Forbes, Julian Codman, and Bob Barlow failed to propagate themselves intellectually, economically, or physically. They were too effete, too genteel, "too well aware of what they would miss." The genteel tradition had had a sympathetic cultural foundation in the economic circles of the Great Merchants. But the new producer's economy beginning to prevail in America during Santayana's youth had inundated the country with a wave of "breakfast foods, shaving soaps, poets, and professors of philosophy." This was an obvious economic and cultural decline, contrasting with the moral and intellectual stability of the old individualistic order.

Two specific friendships emphasized for Santayana the tragedy common to the young men who were unable to find partial solace in Europe. An undergraduate *Lampoon* colleague by the name of

Thomas P. Sanborn, the son of a member of the Emersonian circle, gave Santayana emphatic proof of the ineptness of his generation. Sanborn, a poet, was not in sympathy with the "over-intellectualized transcendentalism of Concord." He sought escape from his heritage in sensuous pleasures. But he awoke, Santayana writes, "bitter and remorseful," in a state of mind that led to suicide. In describing his funeral Santayana is more sarcastic than usual about transcendentalism: "we buried him in Concord, in sight of the optimistic Emerson's grave, after a parlor funeral, with the corpse visible, at which his father read a few not very pertinent passages from the Upanishads and the Psalms."

If suicide was not an inevitable result of the incapacity of these individuals to escape the traditions of their fathers and to meet the demands of their age, then a natural death often came early. Santayana's closest attachment to any American was to his pupil Warwick Potter, who died in 1893, the year of his graduation from Harvard. But Potter's death meant more to Santayana than just another example of a potentially worthwhile American who was physically or mentally or morally unable to realize his capacities in America. Like Susana, Warwick held for Santayana the "two prerequisities . . . of perfect friendship: capacity to worship and capacity to laugh." These were the two windows "through which the mind took flight and morally escaped from this world." The grief over Potter's death was compounded by Susana's marriage in Spain and the death of Santayana's father—all within a year. By accenting the mutations of life and their effect upon his spirit, this accumulation of decisive events greatly impressed Santayana. He discusses this year as being a *metanoia* in his evaluation of the world and his place in it: "Nothing apparently was much changed in my surroundings, opinions or habits; yet the public world was retreating to a greater distance and taking on a new and more delicate colouring, as if by aerial perspective. I realized it was not my world, but only the world of other people: of all those, at least, and they were a vast majority, who had never understood." At the age of thirty Santayana clearly had emotional as well as intellectual reasons for detaching himself from the mainstream of things, especially things American. His remaining eighteen years at Harvard were truly somnambulistic. He wrote in retrospect in 1936,

"I feel that the last fifteen years of my life in America were a dry season, a time of camping in the desert, with very little manna falling from the sky."

In many of Santayana's young friends there had been the incubus of personal tragedy, an inevitable result of the vicissitudes demanded by the rise of American industrialism. Although a number—like Charles Augustus Strong, who was later Santayana's close acquaintance in Europe—survived the rebuffs of their American environment by escaping it, many were actually physically as well as mentally incapable of fighting against it. Sanborn and Potter had served to emphasize that most could not adapt. Their tragedies were not in their dying young, but in their inability to live lives of their own design in an insensate culture. Along with Sanborn and Potter were Philip Savage, Hugh McCullough, Trumbull Stickney, and Cabot Lodge—all "visibly killed," Santayana says, "by the lack of air to breathe. People individually were kind and appreciative to them, as they were to me," he wrote to William Lyon Phelps; "but the system was deadly, and they hadn't any alternative tradition (as I had) to fall back upon: and of course . . . they hadn't the strength of a great intellectual hero who can stand alone." The fate of these friends illustrated for Santayana the conflict between the genteel idealism of America's past and the merging materialism.

If it seems that Santayana's life in America would by necessity have led him to a one-sided criticism and that of a very small portion of our culture, it must be noted that the individuals he knew best were as close to the original American mentality as could be found. From them he drew the *essence* of Americanism. The American character was so vast that Santayana felt it best to speak of it in parables. His memory of the individual American was expressed in a symbol which he explained to an English audience in 1918 and later included in *Character and Opinion in the United States:*

As it happens, the symbolic American can be made largely adequate to the facts; because, if there are immense differences between individual Americans—for some Americans are black—yet there is a great uniformity in their environment, customs, temper, and thoughts. They have all been uprooted from their several soils and ancestries and plunged together into one vortex, whirling irresistibly in a space otherwise quite empty. To be an American is of itself almost a moral condition, an education, and a career. Hence a single ideal figment can cover a large part of what each American is in his character, and almost the whole of what most Americans are in their social outlook and political judgments.

II

America is predominantly the country to which Santayana turns for evidences of modern, northern culture. He came to think of America—"apart from the genteel tradition"—as a symbol of modernism, "purer in America than elsewhere because less impeded and qualified by survivals of the past." His criticism develops a theory of two Americas: one that is progressive, practical, and mechanistic; the other that is regressive, genteel, and effete. In their separateness they create a cultural void and produce a nation that is ultimately uninterested in the freedom of the individual to explore truth, beauty, or spirit.

Santayana's first widely received comments on America were contained in *Interpretations of Poetry and Religion* (1900), a collection of essays scanning the evolution of religion and literature in Western civilization. Here Santayana sketches the background of the schism in Western culture and lets the poets of the North speak for their civilization. In four essays at the heart of the book he reveals that his criticism of the North and of America as its ultimate expression was firmly rooted in his southern European allegiances. In "The Absence of Religion in Shakespeare" Santayana defends the superiority of Homer and Dante (poets of the South) over Shakespeare (poet of the North). Possessing a "luminous philosophy and . . . well-digested experience," the former "dramatised the universe, and endowed it with the tragic unities." In contrast, "the silence of Shakespeare and his philosophical incoherence have something in them that is still heathen; something that makes us wonder whether the northern mind, even in him, did not remain morose and barbarous at its inmost core."

Nineteenth-century England and America, according to Santayana, constitute the most barbarous civilization in history: for even the comparatively barbaric past had retained at least a vision of "beauty, order, and prefection." The nineteenth-century emphasis on the material left no room for universality in poetry. The poetry of barbarism, represented by the works of Browning and Whitman, yielded a whimsical and flickering retrospective fancy, negative and partial ideals, and a moral strength possessed of "blind and miscellaneous vehemence." Both poets are egotistical and primitive because, like their age, they lacked the guidance of reason. Neither poet attempted to do more than describe experience as it came to him. Whitman, Santayana writes, "has gone back to the innocent style of Adam, when the animals filed before him one by one and he called each of them by its name." Yet Whitman's lack of sophistication had partial justification: it corresponded with the illusions harbored by American liberalism and transcendentalism that the New World was beginning all experience over again.

Browning and Whitman proved to Santayana that in the nineteenth century the growing order in the spheres of science and industry was paralleled by a growing chaos in the sphere of the imagination. To Santayana, who believed in revolutions of culture, this was a natural circumstance. But the only criterion for progress, in his view, is the perfecting of the imaginative sphere—the perfection of language, art, and religion. An age in which moral decay is taking place relies on "energy and actuality" to console it for its regression to "sensation and passion." A truly rational age imposes its molds of thought upon Nature; "and the conviction of a definite truth arises together with the vision of a supreme perfection. It is only at such periods," Santayana concludes, "that the human animal vindicates his title of rational." If such an age is to supervene in future generations, it will look back to Whitman and Browning as having been spokesmen for a primitive, material, emotional, and inconclusive age.

If Whitman was successful in catching some of the tendencies of his age and country, he could never be successful in his goal of poet for the American people. Santayana writes that both the sophistication of the American Commonwealth and the decline of the pioneer spirit left his poems high and dry, to be read only by the dilettantes and foreigners who search for the grotesque in their definitions of America. The American people denied Whitman, Santayana thinks, because they held to an ideal of perfection, not to the "corrupt desire to be primitive." But nineteenth-century America produced another poet who spoke the language of the ideal. In his essay on Emerson, Santayana wrote that Emerson was more the puritan mystic than the philosopher. Endowed with "poetic fancy and a gift for observation and epigram," Emerson idealized the laws of Nature, seeing in them an "intelligible form of the divinity he had always recognized and adored." Yet because he was a mystic, Emerson, like Whitman, was not of his time. He was late-born, like Oliver Alden of *The Last Puritan.* While retaining the "moral intensity and metaphysical abstraction" of puritanism, he had foregone its doctrine and had become a Unitarian. "Emerson," writes Santayana, "was indeed the Psyche of Puritanism, 'the latest-born and fairest vision far' of all that 'faded hierarchy.' A Puritan whose religion was all poetry, a poet whose only pleasure was thought, he showed in his life and personality the meagreness, the constraint, the frigid and conscious consecration which belonged to his clerical ancestors, while his inmost impersonal spirit ranged abroad over the fields of history and Nature, gathering what ideas it might, and singing its little snatches of inspired song." Emerson did not degenerate like Oliver, because he had the strength to live in the spirit, feeling no compulsion to live in the world. Although he was involved belatedly in antislavery campaigns and interested in the progress of his country, he was detached from the world because "his heart was fixed on eternal things." Like the Hindus, Persians, Platonists, and Stoics, Santayana writes (using the words of Matthew Arnold), Emerson remained "a friend and aider of those who would live in the spirit."

Neither Emerson nor Whitman spoke for their age, although each, in Santayana's opinion, expressed certain tendencies within it: the one its barbarity and primitiveness, the other its refinement and idealism. Yet the capacity was lacking in both to unite the physical with the spiritual or the real with the ideal. In "A Religion of Disillusion" Santayana turns to the Greeks for his example and tells how this might be done. It is in man's power, he says, to discover by the use of reason the harmony in life. But man must first understand himself in order to achieve the objects of his "rational desire." The process, Santayana writes, is for us "to make a modest inventory of our possessions and a just estimate of our powers in order to apply both, with what strength we have, to the realization of our ideals in society, in art, and in science. These will constitute the Cosmos. In building it—for there is none other that builds it for us—we shall be carrying on the work of the only race that has yet seriously attempted to live rationally, the race to which we owe the name and the idea of a Cosmos, as well as the beginnings of its realization. We shall then be making that rare advance in wisdom which consists of abandoning our illusions the better to attain our ideals." Both primitivism and mysticism failed in the nineteenth century to give a rational basis to the northern liberalism in America.

In the twelve years following *Interpretations of Poetry and Religion* Santayana solidified his philosophical position in two major works, the five-volume *The Life of Reason: or, The Phases of Human Progress* (1905–06) and *Three Philosophical Poets: Lucretius, Dante, and Goethe* (1910). Neither work deals directly with the North or the United States. Each expresses, however, the philosophical reasons for Santayana's discontent with an age unable to live in the mind. *The Life of Reason* is Santayana's extended definition of reason in common sense, society, religion, art, and science. He writes that the reasoning faculty is produced biologically, having its roots in instinct. But as the highest faculty of man it is that "part of experience which perceives and pursues ideals—all conduct so controlled and all sense so interpreted as to perfect natural happiness." Thus the Life of Reason is a prerequisite for an enlightened civilization: "Reason and humanity begin with the union of instinct and ideation, when instinct becomes enlightened, establishes values in its objects, and is turned from a process into an art, while at the same time consciousness becomes practical and cognitive, beginning to contain some symbol or record of the co-ordinate realities among which it arises." In *Three Philosophical Poets* Santayana found the Life of Reason best exemplified by pre-Platonic Greek materialists. Dantean supernaturalism and Goethean romanticism were attritions of the age of reason. In both of these works, which were delivered as lectures to Harvard undergraduates (*Three Philosophical Poets* was also delivered at Columbia and the University of Wisconsin), the first generation of the twentieth century was afforded strong evidence that its predecessors had abandoned the Life of Reason for a more worldly and primitive existence.

It is fitting that Santayana's last academic duty as an American resident was to deliver an address entitled "The Genteel Tradition in American Philosophy" before the Philosophical Union of the University of California. From Boston Santayana had looked out on practical and industrial America and had remarked on its cultural aridity. But in 1911, with the expanse of a continent between him and New England and with the prospect of leaving America close at hand, he turned his complete attention to the condition of the American Intellect. Santayana indicates how wide the gap between the American mind and the American will had become. There are, he says, two mentalities in America: "one a survival of the beliefs and standards of the fathers, the other an expression of the instincts, practice, and discoveries of the younger generations." Thus the things of the mind—religion, literature, and moral emotion—fail to meet the demands of the present. "The truth is," Santayana writes,

that one-half of the American mind, that not occupied intensely in practical affairs, has remained, I will not say high-and-dry, but slightly becalmed; it has floated gently in the back-water, while, alongside, in invention and industry and social organisation, the other half of the mind was leaping down a sort of Niagara Rapids. This division may be found symbolised in American architecture: a neat reproduction of the colonial mansion—with some modern comforts introduced surrep-titiously—stands beside the sky-scraper. The American Will inhabits the sky-scraper; the American Intellect inhabits the colonial mansion. The one is the sphere of the American man; the other, at least predominantly, of the American woman. The one is all aggressive enterprise; the other is all genteel tradition.

The American successes in matters economic and social had destroyed the vitality of both Calvinism and transcendentalism: in the one its "agonized conscience," in the other its "radical subjective criticism of knowledge." The academic mind, Santa-yana tells us, was left with a moral code and an emphasis on the human efficacy of discovering truth which had lost their only means of justification. By renouncing the conditions which made their philosophy vital, American intellectuals could not cope—indeed, had refused to cope—with the practical realities of their times.

In his lecture Santayana pointed to a middle ground emerg-ing in the hiatus between practical and genteel America. He singles out Poe, Hawthorne, and Emerson as nineteenth-century geniuses who could not "retail" the genteel tradition. But their subjectivism, he says, left them "morbid, or tinkling, or self-indulgent," unable to convince others of the vacancy of gentility. Not until the end of the century was the tradition challenged openly. Santayana saw Walt Whitman's Bohemian attack on the

genteel tradition as the beginning of its dissolution. But Whitman's poetry was only a disintegration of accepted standards; it
reduced man to the primitive and failed to provide him with a
positive future. Both Henry and William James, on the other
hand, were more serious threats to the tradition because origi-
nally they were products of it. Henry succeeded in escaping it in
the classic manner, by analyzing it in his novels. William was an
even more formidable foe of the tradition. In championing dissident philosophies, in acknowledging the practical uses of science,
and in viewing the universe as vitalistic, without a "predetermined goal," the "impassioned empiricism" of William
James had "broken the spell of the genteel tradition."[5]

"The Genteel Tradition in American Philosophy" was
published as the last chapter of a collection of essays entitled
Winds of Doctrine: Studies in Contemporary Opinion (1913),
which Santayana began compiling almost as soon as he left
America in January 1912. As George Howgate wrote in 1938, the
book "somehow suggests the pulling up of old roots in the author's life, the burning of bridges which have been crossed, the
emergence from the academic cloister of a man of the larger,
outer world." The doctrines are varied: besides the essay on the
genteel tradition, there is a survey of the intellectual temper of
the age, an essay on modernism and Christianity, papers on
Bergson and Russell, and a favorable criticism of Shelley. De-
spite a surface inconsistency, the unity of the book is achieved by
Santayana's continual return to the Life of Reason as ballast
against the variable winds of doctrine.

"The Intellectual Temper of the Age" charts the winds of
doctrine which Santayana felt were prevailing in the North at the
time of his departure from America. The age, he writes, still had
an affinity for traditional religion, art, politics, and moral codes;
but Christendom was being challenged by "the unconquerable
mind of the East, the pagan past, the industrial socialistic

---

[5] It is interesting that Santayana complimented his audience on their own
escape from the genteel tradition by their absorption in the grandeurs of
coastal scenery. But he was obviously disappointed in their lack of intellectual life. In 1911 he wrote to his sister Susana, "What I have seen in
California and Canada . . . has left no impression on my mind whatever.
They are intellectually emptier than the Sahara, where I understand the
Arabs have some idea of God or of Fate."

future. . . ." A new spirit was slowly filtering upward—"that of an emancipated, atheistic, international democracy." American liberalism, so optimistic at the turn of the century, was weakened, not because it lacked the will to progress, but because it had forgotten its aims. He complains that

> those who speak most of progress measure it by quantity and not by quality; how many people read and write, or how many people there are, or what is the annual value of their trade; whereas true progress would rather lie in reading or writing fewer and better things, and being fewer and better men, and enjoying life more. But the philanthropists are now preparing an absolute subjection of the individual, in soul and body, to the instincts of the majority—the most cruel and unprogressive of masters; and I am not sure that the liberal maxim "the greatest happiness of the greatest number," has not lost whatever was just or generous in its intent and come to mean the greatest idleness of the largest possible population.

His conservatism notwithstanding, Santayana did not bemoan the new reform that he saw in the movement from liberalism to socialism and "in love of nature, athletics, in the new woman, and in a friendly medical attitude towards all the passions." Change is a part of the inevitable process of social evolution; and the reform, he believed, would be integrative and creative, whereas the existing liberalism was not. But in matters of the intellect (fine arts, religion, and philosophy), stagnation, even disintegration, prevailed. Nineteenth-century romanticism, "half lurid, half effeminate," supplanted by "a brutal pursuit of material truth," resulted in a cultural anarchy that had not been overcome.

Where then lay the hope of the age? Santayana turns again to his plea that man live in the mind. But contemporary intellectuals, possessed of only enough intelligence to show them their errors, turned as did Whitman to something further back in the evolutionary process. Of their misconception of the Life of Reason, Santayana says,

> In the presence of such cruelly confused things as theology [the present age] feels *la nostalgie de la boue*. It was only, M. Bergson tells us, where dead matter oppressed life that life was forced to become intelligence; for this reason intelligence kills whatever it touches; it is the tribute life pays to death. . . . Finding their intelligence enslaved, our contemporaries suppose that intelligence is essentially servile; instead of freeing it, they try to elude it. Not free enough themselves morally, but bound to the world partly by piety and partly by industrialism, they cannot think of rising to a detached

contemplation of earthly things, and of life itself and evolution; they revert rather to sensibility, and seek some by-path of instinct or dramatic sympathy in which to wander. Having no stomach for the ultimate, they burrow downwards towards the primitive. But the longing to be primitive is a disease of culture; it is archaism in morals. To be so preoccupied with vitality is a symptom of anae-mia. . . . Nothing can be meaner than the anxiety to live on, to live on anyhow and in any shape; a spirit with any honour is not willing to live except in its own way, and a spirit with any wisdom is not over eager to live at all.

Again Santayana had to refer to pre-Platonic Greece for an example of true intellectual vitality, which through the Life of Reason found materialism and idealism compatible.

Santayana concludes his essay by accusing the North of forfeit-ing the Life of Reason for cruder powers. In modernism, pragma-tism, and the philosophy of Bergson, reason was used only to make its users feel superior. On the other hand, Santayana notes, there are a few individuals in every age who employ reason to aid them in retiring from the world—as Shelley did in the nine-teenth century (without really knowing it) and as Bertrand Russell and Santayana himself did in 1913—because they "feel that the sphere of what happens to exist is too alien and acciden-tal to absorb all the play of a free mind, whose function, after it has come to clearness and made its peace with things, is to touch them with its own moral and intellectual light, and to exist for its own sake."

Winds of Doctrine reasserted the standards by which Santa-yana judged his American experience. His opinons of the North were little altered by the time he left America: America and the North were both changing in a way he had foreseen. Within six years of *Winds of Doctrine* there was a singular defeat of *Kultur* in Germany, a radical test of liberalism in America, and the establishment of socialism in Russia. Yet, if in America new philosophical winds were blowing favorably on the American Will, the American Intellect still sailed principally by the gusts of mild New England zephyrs. The America Santayana left was still a country of two mentalities.

Character and Opinion in the United States: With Reminis-cences of William James and Josiah Royce and Academic Life in America (1920) retraces much of the ground Santayana had followed in earlier criticism of America, but it recognizes funda-

mental changes in the American scene. The fact that the essays
were written for a British audience six to eight years after Santayana had left America gives to them a reflective, detached tone.
In the preface he explains, "I try to understand [the heart of
America], as a family friend may who has a different temperament; but it is only my mind that I speak for at bottom, or wish
to speak for." The first essay, "The Moral Background," recasts
the argument of "The Genteel Tradition in American Philosophy," outlining the development of America's genteel intellect
and showing its gradual disassociation from the progressive life
of America. The essay opens with a metaphor comparing the
mid-nineteenth-century mind to a brilliant Indian summer, which
resulted only in a harvest of leaves. American artists and thinkers
(he refers to Bryant and Longfellow) "lacked native roots and
sap because the American intellect itself lacked them. Their
culture," he continues, "was half a pious survival, half an intentional acquirement; it was not the inevitable flowering of a fresh
experience." Nineteenth-century Unitarianism and economics favored this mind. It was the period of the Great Merchants, when
"material restlessness was not yet ominous, the pressure of business enterprises was not yet out of scale with the old life or out of
key with the old moral harmonies. A new type of American had
not appeared—the untrained, pushing, cosmopolitan orphan,
cock-sure in manner but not too sure in his morality, to whom the
old Yankee, with his sour integrity, is almost a foreigner." This
placidity of mind entered the twentieth century transformed and
attenuated, Santayana says, because cut off from the stream of
human progress. The orthodoxy that American intellectuals carried into the twentieth century "consisted in holding that the
universe exists and is governed for the sake of man or of the
human spirit." For Santayana, this type of intellect admits of
impotence, substituting "habit and moral presumption" for the
more balanced perspectives of reason. Only the Greeks "at their
best . . . ," Santayana writes, "realized the sweetness and glory
of being a rational animal." Meanwhile, the humanists, although
holding to "solemn and venerable" systems, were experiencing a
growing insecurity. Incursions into the academic world were
being made by naturalists such as William James. But naturalism
as yet lacked a concerted movement. Like James, American naturalists were uncomfortable in their ideas because they "worried

about what *ought* to be believed and the awful deprivations of disbelieving." Moreover, they, too, lacked an appeal to their age; for they studied only what interested them individually. Like the genteel tradition—but for opposing reasons—they failed to see the relation of mankind to Nature.

How these ideas were retailed by the academic mind during his own tenure at Harvard from about 1885 to 1910 is the subject of "The Academic Environment," "William James," and "Josiah Royce." Neither American public nor private education has produced original thinkers, according to Santayana. The American life dissolves the toughest and most alien intellectual elements into "the native good-will, complacency, thoughtlessness, and optimism." At Harvard itself, the professors could think what they liked, but it had to be consecrated "to the common task of encouraging everybody and helping everything on." Even atheism was almost tolerated; but "the atmosphere was not that of intelligence nor of science, it was that of duty." Harvard philosophy was of the place and the hour. Even the great teachers like Royce and James were faced with the problem of describing things as they are while at the same time trying to fit those things into the preconceived desires of society. In his essays on them, Santayana shows respect for their characters and methods; but he questions the motives of their thought. Within the same department there existed the radical empiricism and pragmatism of James and the idealism and transcendentalism of Royce. In a free culture this would have been a healthy state of affairs. But both philosophies were drawn from Calvinism, and neither philosopher was able to relate his philosophy to human life. Santayana even denies that any of the Harvard professors had a notion of the "good life": "They had much experience of personal goodness, and love of it; they had standards of character and right conduct; but as to what might render human existence good, excellent, beautiful, happy, and worth having as a whole, their notions were utterly thin and barbarous. They had forgotten the Greeks, or never known them."

In "Later Speculations" (a modification of a lecture entitled "Philosophical Opinion in America," delivered in 1918 to the British Academy) Santayana again felt the weakening pulse of the genteel tradition, which had weathered almost two decades of the twentieth century. He denies that *polite* America had

developed anything original in philosophy or letters, but had
only followed a tradition of Christendom parallel to that followed by England. But perhaps in deference to his British audience he adds that its character is different from that produced by
the European intellect because America's great distance had
produced in it "in-breeding and anaemia." Alongside this weakened gentility he recognizes a "crude but vital America" which is
"undermining, feeding, and transforming the America of tradition." This is Santayana's old distinction between the two Americas, now modified slightly with the passage of time. The new
philosophers frankly embrace the external world. They have broken through the bar that kept James and Royce from uniting the
mental with the physical life. Santayana calls this new breed of
American philosopher "a cell in that teeming democratic society."
Unlike the pragmatists and idealists from which he descended,
he is a professional and a technician. The new realists turned the
conventional categories of philosophy into an unprejudiced discussion of all ideas. So successful were they that Santayana
remarks, "Never was the human mind master of so many facts
and sure of so few principles." American philosophy remained
without form. It wanted only a genius with imagination and
moral heroism who could formulate the "vast collection of suggestions" and "the radical analysis of presumptions." If this
should happen, Santayana concludes, "We may be frightened at
first to learn on what thin ice we have been skating, in specula-
tion as in government; but we shall not be in a worse plight for
knowing it, only wiser to-day and perhaps safer to-morrow."

In "Materialism and Idealism in American Life" Santayana
questioned whether the new spirit of America would remain
materialistic or whether it contained the potential to achieve a
mature idealism. The business of settling a continent had limited
the American to a moral materialism that went "hand in hand
with present contentment and with foresight of what the future
very likely will bring." Lacking the time to live in the mind,
Americans learned to use quantity as a justification for lack of
quality in their achievements, whereas the moral idealism of
poets and artists—an idealism still in abeyance in America—
would be more consonant with man's happiness. Moral idealism
consists, Santayana explains, of the capacity "to be poor in order
to be simple, to produce less in order that the product may be
more choice and beautiful and may leave us less burdened with

unnecessary duties and useless possessions—that is an ideal not articulate in the American mind; yet here and there I seem to have heard a sigh after it, a groan at the perpetual incubus of business and shrill society. Significant witness to such aspirations is borne by those new forms of popular religion, not mere variations on tradition, which have sprung up from the soil—revivalism, spiritualism, Christian Science, the New Thought." But Santayana does not despair of America. The American, he writes, is still young: "he is chiefly occupied with his immediate environment" and "his reactions upon it are inwardly prompted, spontaneous, and full of vivacity and self-trust. His views are not yet lengthened; his will is not yet broken or transformed." He possesses a natural idealism that—if ever faced by "serious and irremediable tribulation"—may yet mature and become a moral freedom. The American then may begin to realize the value of "things that are pure good in themselves, so that once to have found and loved them, whatever else may betide, may remain a happiness that nothing can sully."

This confidence in the resurgent vitality of America is also the subject of the final essay, "English Liberty in America," which traces the spirit of free cooperation in America back to the instinct for free individuality in the English inner man. Along with the will to work and to prosper, the spirit of cooperation is, for Santayana, "the essence of Americanism." In moral terms it resembles liberalism. For instance, the suburbanite who attends to business in the city is the victim of long hours of work, hasty meals, and sweltering trains with no time "to exist morally at all." Even the best of American life is compulsory:

the idealism, the zeal, the beautiful happy unison of its great moments. You must wave, you must cheer, you must push with the irresistible crowd; otherwise you will feel like a traitor, a soulless outcast, a deserted ship high and dry on the shore. In America there is but one way of being saved, though it is not peculiar to any of the official religions, which themselves must silently conform to the national orthodoxy, or else become impotent and merely ornamental. This national faith and morality are vague in idea, but inexorable in spirit; they are the gospel of work and the belief in progress. By them, in a country where all men are free, every man finds that what most matters has been settled beforehand.

Yet even when it compels conformity, this liberty is better than the primitive cries of absolute freedom made by fanatics, martyrs, poets, doctrinaires, and dilettantes. For the conservative

Santayana, primitive freedom is a heresy against the laws of Nature and doomed to be transitory. English liberty is in harmony with the nature of things, keeping the mass of individual passions in check by mutual agreement and by exercise of the Life of Reason, while absolute liberty is "incompatible with more than one pulse of life." America finds its best heritage in liberty based on union. Without it, Santayana warns, "liberty loses its massiveness, its plasticity, its power to survive change; it ceases to be tentative and human in order to become animal and absolute."

Character and Opinion in the United States may be regarded as Santayana's final comment on the America with which he was familiar. Even his novel deals with events no later than World War I. The essays were compiled during his stay in wartime England, while his American residence was still fresh in his mind and while the many American soldiers he met reminded him of the American spirit. But as the distance in time widened and as new interests came to the fore, his criticism of America seemed limited to occasional pieces, his letters, and his novel. Yet the next decade was probably his most productive as a scholar and essayist, a fact which by itself justifies Santayana's resignation from Harvard and America so that he might be free to pursue the life of the mind for which he had waited half a century. He collected the opinions he had formed while in England in *Soliloquies in England* (1922) and initiated his second major philosophical treatise with *Scepticism and Animal Faith* (1923), followed by the first two volumes of the four-volume *The Realms of Being* in 1927 and 1930. In the meantime he himself went to the Greeks in *Dialogues in Limbo* (1925) and proved his versatility by publishing a revised selection of poetry in 1923 and a second edition of his tragedy *Lucifer* in 1924.

In the two decades following his departure from America, Santayana had witnessed the defeat of the genteel tradition at the hands of the liberals in the academic ranks, and he had blessed the insurgents; for they at least possessed the vital interest in their country so lacking before in the academic mind.[6] But

---

[6] Santayana's blessing was mixed, however. His own denunciation of the genteel tradition in 1911 had anticipated such dissident commentaries as that of Van Wyck Brooks in *America's Coming of Age* (1915) and Ran-

the genteel tradition was not dead, even when Santayana was writing its epitaph in *Character and Opinion in the United States*. For two reasons its revitalization in the writings of Baker Brownell, Irving Babbitt, Paul Elmer More, and Stuart Pratt Sherman (under the banner of new-humanism) brought Santayana to a fresh analysis of it. In the first place, he still considered it to have an enervating effect on American culture. In the second, because of his classical bent, he had been called a new-humanist himself; and he sought to deny this. Three essays published in the *Saturday Review* and later collected as *The Genteel Tradition at Bay* (1931) serve as a summation of all that Santayana had written on America as a product of the northern mind, of its cultural schism, and of its only hope in the Life of Reason.

In "The Analysis of Modernity" he warns that the new-humanism is not the soft Renaissance variety of the nineteenth century which ended in a "pensive agnosticism" and a "charmed culture" with Matthew Arnold. The new-humanists protest against this end and are prepared to do battle with modernism, a modernism now secure in the bastions of American Big Business. Modern man, he writes, is a product of all the anarchical movements in the past five hundred years: the Renaissance, the Reformation, Revolution, and Romance. The result is "a many-sided insurrection of the unregenerate man, with all his physical powers and affinities, against the regimen of Christendom." The modern man of Big Business denies that physical life is a life of sin or misery. Society is given over to material achievements which world crises seem to abet. Even if economic difficulties and spiritual distress still abound, Big Business and its subsidiaries such as the mechanical arts and abstract science promote "ambition, cooperation, and rivalry" which "keep the snowball rolling and getting bigger and bigger." For the present at least, public order is able to keep private anarchy in control. In doing so, modernism has provided virtue and happiness for the individ-

---

dolph Bourne in *Youth and Life* (1913) and *The History of a Literary Radical* (1920). But Santayana himself was unwilling to accept what he felt was an unalloyed negativism on the part of the insurgents: he clearly distinguishes his position in "America's Young Radicals" and in "Marginal Notes on *Civilization in the United States*," the final two essays of this book.

ual, who is "invited to share an industrious, cordial, sporting
existence, self-imposed and self-rewarding."

The success of Big Business, Santayana concludes, threatens
the role of the new-humanist. It too could end like the Renaissance humanism of Arnold, "expiring of fatigue, or evaporating
into a faint odour of learning and sentiment hanging about Big
Business." On the other hand, he says that it has an opportunity
to become an effectual cultural force by returning to its sources
in Calvinism, which was "not essentially humanistic at all, but
theocratic." Theocracy would be the new-humanists' only method
of doing effective battle with a society nursed in the Renaissance,
Revolution, Reformation, and Romance. Santayana gives warning
to the new-humanists: "Culture won't do, they must say, unless it
be the one right culture: learning won't do unless it fills out the
one true philosophy. No more sentimentality, then, or intellectual
snobbery; away with the sunset glow and the organ peals over-
heard in a churchyard. Let us have honest bold dogmas supported by definite arguments; let us re-establish our moral sentiments on foundations more solid than tradition or gentility."

A return to Calvinism would be a frank acceptance of supernaturalism. And in "The Appeal to Supernaturalism" Santayana
describes this as the only way in which the new-humanists can
uphold an absolute criterion of taste and morals. Christian Pla-
tonism is the supernatural system which lies nearest at hand, in
that it is already "remarkably humanistic" and "deifies morality
and human intelligence."[7] But if this is the way the new-
humanists hope to gain strength for their absolutism, it is not
sound for the naturalist Santayana. The detached philosopher
cannot admit that the universe is "nothing but an enlarged edi-

---

[7] By 1931 Santayana had good reason to speak forthrightly about the
gravitation of new-humanism to supernaturalism. He was not just offering a
prescription for a potential movement in new-humanism; he was describing
a movement already begun. Irving Babbitt, his former colleague and the
high priest of new-humanism, had said in an essay defining humanism in
Norman Foerster's *Humanism and America* (1930) that religion might be
the matrix for the moral self-hood for which new-humanism had been
searching. And in 1928 Santayana's former pupil T. S. Eliot had announced
that he was an Anglo-Catholic in religion. Also in 1928, Eliot had written of
humanism's alliance with supernaturalism in "The Humanism of Irving
Babbitt" in terms much like those used by Santayana: "the humanistic point
of view is auxiliary to and dependent upon the religious point of view."

tion, or an expurgated edition, of human life." For Santayana, human nature includes intelligence and cannot be perfected without the illumination and equipoise intelligence gives. Although the regimen "sanctified by Platonic and Christian moralists" is not unacceptable, it is illusory: "they simply received back from revelation the humanism which they had put into it."

In "The Moral Adequacy of Naturalism" Santayana argues for a natural ground for morality—"the principle of all choices in taste, faith, and allegiance." The Life of Reason discovers that the living organism cannot go beyond what is natural: "As the brute unconditionally wills to live, so the man, especially the strong masterful man, unconditionally wills to live after a certain fashion. To be pliant, to be indefinite, seems to him ignominious." The Life of Reason also allows for more variety than either liberalism or moral absolutism. It does not "prescribe the girth of a man, or his stature; it can only reveal to his imperfect self his possible perfection." Moreover, naturalism should not be considered as favorable only to the lower sides of human nature: it can attain to the insights of supernaturalism. "It is essential," Santayana maintains, "to the validity of a moral maxim that it should be framed in the interest of natural impulses." For American humanists to find sanctions for their moral absolutism in the supernatural, then, is an escape from the use of intelligence. At best all that the new-humanists can do is to offer to mankind the way of Matthew Arnold or of Charles Eliot Norton. Santayana denies his allegiance to such a system: "No true appreciation of any thing is possible without a sense of its naturalness, of the innocent necessity by which it has assumed its special and perhaps extraordinary form. In a word, the principle of morality is naturalistic. Call it humanism or not, only a morality frankly relative to man's nature is worthy of man, being at once vital and rational, martial and generous; whereas absolutism smells of fustiness as well as faggots."

Finally, Santayana's naturalism more than ever controls and directs his estimate of America in the last two decades of his life. He grows increasingly doubtful that America can achieve an organic culture. His novel *The Last Puritan* dramatizes the failure of American culture to become self-sustaining. The life of Oliver Alden illustrates a serious but ineffectual attempt by sensitive young American intellectuals of the early twentieth century to provide a culture commensurate with the achievements of a mechanized society. Possessing the legacy of puritanism themselves, they were dissatisfied with its precipitant, the genteel tradition. But the conditions of that legacy prevented them from uniting with the vital American Will and redirecting that Will from preoccupation with the control of matter to reflection on the consequences of its control. In a "mechanized democracy" content with its physical successes, there was no function for young intellectuals who inherited the "agonized conscience" of their forebears. Santayana saw the atavistic puritan as a tragic figure—full of noble intentions but lacking the vigor to effect them. Ralph Barton Perry says that Santayana's novel defines the death of the puritan creed in America. This death, he writes, "resembles the death of any creed when its subordinations have become negations, its conventions rigidities, and its surviving zealots monstrosities." Even if this is true, Santayana does not discount the puritan contribution to both the Will and the Intellect in America. For him puritanism is the only identifiable tradition there is in America. But on the intellectual side in either pristine or genteel form, it has become effete. Like Hamlet and Faust, Santayana's puritan is a Nordic who suffers from self-delusion and lack of direction.

Santayana pleads for an organic American culture, the matrix being the mechanistic society which is at present so insensate to cultural development. He maintains that the dialogue that will educate the American Will should not be between itself and the American Intellect but between the Will and the detached and contemplative mind of the Mediterranean-Catholic South. In an essay entitled "Americanism" (published in 1957 in Daniel Cory's collection *The Idler and His Works*), Santayana writes that physical domination over Nature can result in only a primitive civilization. He exclaims, "What irony there would be in having learned to control matter, if we thereby forgot the purposes of the soul in controlling it, and disowned the natural furniture of the mind, our senses, fancy, and pictorial knowledge!" From his southern European heritage he has learned that "the great part of human life, by a biological necessity, must always be carried on in terms of sense, passion, and language." If science and industry are to be useful, they must be made subservient to the Life of

Reason that understands the value of the human soul. Otherwise, he concludes, it would be fatal for mechanized America to dominate reason and substitute "blind work for free imagination." Out of its primitivism America has the potential to establish the arts "in such a way that they are practiced intelligibly and that they yield agreeable fruits."

During his long life, Santayana never found evidence that the American Will and the American Intellect had united to form a common, organic culture. When speaking of modern America in the fifties, Santayana does not even discuss the American Intellect, an indication that he felt it had faded from importance almost entirely. And he believes that in "manners and sentiment" the American Will is "so continuous and monotonous as to become automatic." Further, in *Dominations and Powers: Reflections on Liberty, Society, and Government* (1951), he writes that the post–World War II American psyche is unlike the "human psyche" of the "few and idealistic" pre–Civil War New England sages who had "a seminal bent, a spontaneous inner proclivity, often an originality and turn for invention." These ancestors of Oliver Alden had been "overwhelmed by the major current, into which they themselves wished to pass; and they were increasingly subdued to the colour of what they worked in, and hailed as prophets of the brave new world that was taking shape in complete disregard of their private spirits." Santayana can still praise modern American liberalism's efforts for peace and economic stability; but he wonders about the consequences if American philanthropic liberalism should impart its culture to other nations along with its goods. American culture, he implies, having suffered from failure of its intellectuals, has not yet become organic. The American Will has still not developed the life of the mind. In a final essay in *Dominations and Powers* entitled "The United States as Leader" he warns nations about submitting themselves unconditionally to the philanthropic zeal of the American Will: "By the obvious well-being which they bring, they breed self-satisfaction and complacency . . . . The authority that controlled universal economy, if it were in American hands, would irresistibly tend to control education and training also. . . . The philanthropic passion for service would prompt social, if not legal, intervention in the traditional life of all other nations, not only by selling there innumerable

American products, but by recommending, if not imposing, American ways of living and thinking."

For Santayana, post–World War II America does not contain the puritan ethos of which Oliver Alden was the last and most essential representative. America has lost its cultural identity; or else its cultural identity has been vitiated and absorbed by an alien cultural force which has not yet learned to understand itself. The life of the mind ossified with the puritan conscience and disintegrated with the American intellectual's attempts to meet the conditions imposed upon him by the American Will. What is left is the American Will still in its barbaric state, not yet aware of its own identity, and unable, so far, to realize its potential to cultivate that identity. It is from the classical naturalist rather than from the late-born puritan that the American Will can learn to liberate its "native potentialities." In the essay "Americanism" Santayana insists that America must cease to be merely physical—a condition of inorganic matter—and become both intellectual and moral. "Mechanistic democracy" can emerge from its primitive state only by becoming organic, by effecting a life that is "vital, perfect, and appropriate." Life, Santayana asserts, "should be *vital*, that is, fed by sap rising from its hereditary root, spontaneously, gladly, freely. A life should also be *perfect*, that is, harmonious with itself, and culminating in a distinct form or order in which all the parts are included without being distorted. Finally, life should be *appropriate;* that is, capable of maintaining itself and feeding on its surroundings, by adopting for its vitality a type of perfection which circumstances render possible at that particular time and place."

Part I

PERSONS AND PLACES

Editor's note: The Background of My Life and *The Middle Span,* the first two volumes of the three-volume autobiography *Persons and Places,* tell of Santayana's childhood and early manhood in genteel surroundings. The culture of his early years is evocative not only of another century but of another world, that of a waning Great Merchant society. Although all of the essays in this section describe this world, only "Glimpses of Old Boston" is written, like the autobiography, from a distance in time and space. What one notices most in "Glimpses of Old Boston" is Santayana's power to write symbolically, describing through objects the moral atmosphere of the time and place. But there is also a subtle irony, a mental attitude which pervades most of the essays in this book. His talent for seeing the humor in things led him to be chosen as one of the freshmen editors of *The Harvard Lampoon* in 1883. Interestingly enough, his contribution to the magazine, of which he writes in "The *Lampoon* from 1883 to 1886," was some fifty-three illustrated cartoons. But his humor served him in a private way. It sustained him when he was forced to witness the recurring failure of his friends of high promise. One of these was Thomas Parker Sanborn, of whom he was to write that he "was visibly killed by the lack of air to breathe" in American culture. In Santayana's time this culture reconstituted itself through its institutions. Both "A Glimpse of Yale" and "The Spirit and Ideals of Harvard University" reveal Santayana's capacity to comprehend the exact nature of the most formidable American institutions of his day and to make some startlingly perceptive assessments of the character of American education.

GLIMPSES OF OLD BOSTON

When I search my memory for details about the first issue of *The Latin School Register*, I find a complete blank. The fact is I can have had little to do with it; neither the idea nor the requisite energy could have been mine, and the credit for launching so wonderfully long-lived and prosperous an undertaking must belong entirely to the business manager and the other contributors. I have often written since for other periodicals, and I observe that almost invariably they have soon stopped publication. If the *Register* has kept afloat for fifty years and never got into debt, I am afraid it has not devoted much space to expounding my philosophy.

Now, however, that I have the chance, let me put forward a simple theory of memory, to serve as an apology for any inaccuracies that may have crept into my recollections. Why do we so vividly remember some things and so utterly forget others? Because the traces of some past events are watered, as it were, and kept alive by our present interests; while traces of events which no longer interest us are neglected and allowed to decay, like old

This essay first appeared in *The Latin School Register*, March, 1932. It has been extracted in the *Tercentenary History of the Boston Latin School*, edited by P. Holmes, 1935.

books never dusted and forgotten on the top shelf. In keeping a part of the past alive, however, living imagination tends to transform and embellish it. The facts become incidents in a story, elements in a picture. We drop out all in them that means nothing to us now, and fuse the rest into our general knowledge of the world.

There is one image above all others that survives from the wreckage of my school days: the picture of the old Bedford Street Schoolhouse. There is no beauty in it, and little intrinsic interest; but for me it has become a symbol; a part of one of those Great Companions, one of those friendly worlds or countries of the imagination, which accompany a man through life. They become parts of himself, from which he draws his dreams, or his stories if he is a writer of stories; and in the style of those remembered episodes he may invent others, having the same homely flavour. The Bedford Street Schoolhouse was, or seemed, a vast rickety old shell of a building, bare, shabby, and forlorn to the point of squalor; not dirty exactly, but worn, shaky, and stained deeply in every part by time, weather, and merciless usage. The dingy old brick wall—everything in that world was dingy red brick—had none of those soft pink lights or mossy patina or plastic inequalities of surface which make some old brick walls so beautiful. They remained stark and unyielding in spite of time, thin and sharp like impoverished old maids; and the glassy expanse of those great rattling window-sashes, cut into many panes, and movable with difficulty, remained blank and vacant. No blackboard was black; all were indelibly clouded with ingrained layers of old chalk; the more was rubbed out, the more was rubbed in. Every desk was covered with generations of inkspots, and cut deeply with lines and letters and grotesque drawings. A ramshackle staircase wound up through the heart of the building, to the fourth storey, where the Hall was; and down those steep and dangerous curves the avalanche of nail-hoofed boys would come thundering down, forty or eighty or two hundred together. However short your legs might be, it was simpler and safer to rush down with the avalanche, trusting to luck, rather than to hold back or fall out, and be trampled upon or deserted.

Many later impressions have come to ally themselves in my mind with this image of the old schoolhouse: in the first place the

Harvard of the 1880's still confined to the Yard and the streets immediately adjacent. That too, or the side of it which I saw and lived in, was a red-brick world, mean and shabby-genteel, with an atmosphere of whimsical, ineffectual Bohemia. There the pert, impecunious youth sheltered himself, or even swaggered, in defiance of official window-dressing. Shams may be ancient and powerful, but there is always something more ancient and more powerful, which is reality. There was a certain intellectual heroism in refusing to conform. Later I found the same sentimental Bohemia, in the same red brick setting, still surviving in some circles in England, for instance, in the Inns of Court, and in the more modest corners of Oxford and Cambridge. It was the world of Hogarth and Cruikshank, of Dickens and Thackeray, romantic but sardonic, poetic but inglorious. Something of it seems to persist in the Dublin of James Joyce. Morally there was a sort of interregnum. The Christian system had receded; it stood like a great city church in the midst of business, undemolished but unused. Though you might know nothing about philosophy you were sure that all the philosophies of the past needed to be drastically revised and reversed. Science was a mighty word, the great future of industry loomed vaguely but magnificently before you, and any ulterior rebellion against it, though Ruskin might prophesy it, was put aside as unthinkable. Unthinkable was a favourite word in those days. Wealth and Morality dominated the scene from their granite pedestals, like ponderous Victorian statues: in the shadow of those beneficent powers you grew up miraculously respectable and genteel, like David Copperfield and Oliver Twist. Yet your surroundings sloped sharply down from the demure propriety of home and of the schoolroom (when the teacher was looking) to a tipsy back-alley world of waifs and ne'er-do-wells, where the women (except the young and tender ones) were like Mrs. Gamp, the business men like Mr. Micawber, and the geniuses like Edgar Allan Poe. The same atmosphere, even more concentrated and pungent, prevailed in the old Yankee smoking-car. A villainous but most necessary stove stood, red-hot, in a corner; men in their shirt-sleeves, with hats on the back of their heads, sat chewing and smoking and playing poker with a dirty old pack of cards. But these men could tell good stories, other than their tiresome funny ones. They knew their world thoroughly, and some of them had grand principles and a grand eloquence of the grand old republican sort.

For me, the picturesqueness of this old-fashioned yet so recent world would be enough. It would supply a second series of Dickens' novels not needing to be written, because they were living. Nevertheless, this picturesque modern history has a moral, which I think is that of Dickens also: namely, that human society can get on very well without greatness; that common life suffices, not indeed for greatness, but for love, for laughter, for contentment. I know this is a hard doctrine to preach in Boston: who, there, was ever content to lead a common life and to leave greatness alone? At the Latin School in particular, with our Homer and Virgil, if we had understood them in their moral supremacy, how could we have abstained from following them in sublime flights? In the Hall at the top of those Bedford Street stairs, above the little red-carpeted platform on which we stood for Declamation, a white marble lady with a gracefully curving arm perpetually offered us a wreath of yellow immortelles. As far as I know, however, she never actually placed it on any living boy's head. Perhaps we were wrong in imagining that she was offering that crown to *us*. We should have had to die first. Only our names would have received it.

There were also in the universe other ladies not made of marble. Sometimes a sweet creature would ask you to call. With some trepidation you walked up the handsome flight of brown stone steps that led to the abode of Elegance. You were kept waiting a long time for that imposing door to open. The first time, probably, you hadn't dared to pull the door-bell hard enough, for fear of breaking the wire. Within, all was solemnity and hush: thick carpets drowned your footsteps. Here and there a gas-jet, turned down low, marked the long distances, or dimly revealed the shining surfaces of black-walnut monumental furniture, Chinese vases, and gilded picture-frames. The tables seemed heavy and fixed like sepulchres, and the armchairs grew in their places like separate oaks. You had a terrible feeling that you were not expected and not wanted; the simplicity and naturalness of the inmates, when finally one or two appeared, surprised and reassured you. These ladies were gentle, they were witty, above all they were kind; yet somehow you felt that you had interrupted their nap, that they had changed their clothes and smoothed their hair before coming down to receive you. Moreover, you were sure they would have received anybody else with the same sweetness and the same civility. No, you didn't call again.

All this was fifty or sixty years ago. As Nero found Rome brick and left it marble, so the generation now passing away found Boston an old Yankee seaport, spread out quietly over two or three hillsides, round two or three conspicuous steeples and the State House dome: all plain brick or painted brick or brick faced with stone, still interspersed with wooden shanties and vacant lots, among which the tinkling horse-car would jog by every half-hour; and they have left Boston—as you see it to-day. They found, or they founded the *Register*, an amateurish little sheet of four pages, full of would-be jokes, misprints, and boyish silliness; and they left it this serious, mature, many-sided, informative, illustrated literary magazine which the reader holds admiringly in his hand.

THE LAMPOON FROM
1883 TO 1886

When Ibis, in the pleasant disguise of Frederick Nichols, knocked at the door of 19 Hollis and announced to its humble occupant, a witless Freshman, that he had been crowned with the cap and bells, there were already in the *Lampoon* Board two members of the Class of '86. Alas, they were not destined long to survive their separation from it. Their three or four years with Lampy, and the briefness of their later careers, give them an eminent right to be identified with his history. They were T. P. Sanborn and C. C. Felton. The first brought from the oracular shades of Concord a fine wit and sensibility, which could bend at times to the indicting of little lyrics for the printer's devil—things in which college life was touched at its edges, and in which the poetic soul, not quite at ease in its somewhat ungainly body and arid surroundings, found vent in slight overtones of fancy and tenderness. Felton, on the other hand, was a wit of the masculine and squelching kind, and drew for the pages of the Only Successful cartoons somewhat in the manner since adopted by the professional colored press. His chum, W. W. Baldwin, soon joined our forces, and we four, who used to dine at the same

Santayana contributed this essay to *Reminiscences and a List of Editors of the Harvard Lampoon, 1876–1901,* privately printed at Cambridge, 1901.

table in Memorial, formed what I may call the nucleus of the '86 Board—a nucleus around which very little else gathered until our college course was nearly at its end.

Thayer I, where Baldwin and Felton lived, was our chief stamping ground, and there pages were composed on which posterity, if it chose, might confer immortality. We had no methods but those of Art and Bohemia. The Business Editor alone took a serious and responsible view of the situation. The rest of us cultivated a philosophic disbelief in space and time. The numbers were always late and not always funny. When a critical moment approached and something had to be done about the next issue, we held a joint meeting of an evening in Thayer I. Felton would illustrate his own jokes; I would strive to clothe in the latest fashions such episodes with girls in them as the general inventiveness could supply me with; while Sanborn would edit a "By the Way," also inspired by the Universal Consciousness, and Baldwin, to keep us all up to a classic standard, would read us Thackeray or the Decameron, or something else which, if Lampy had had a library, ought to have been found there. A library, or rather a Sanctum, was indeed provided for Lampy when the generous hand of Billy Hearst held the purse-strings. It was a room in Brattle Street, with a carpet and a genuinely American stove, but with a concession in favor of the French comic papers, to broaden the mind. This new splendor, however, did not change our homely habits, and Thayer I remained the workshop and lounging-place of unpampered genius. I believe the Brattle Street Sanctum did not outlast the transit of Hearst through our heavens, on his way to that higher sphere where he is now shining.

Those were not yet the days of tit-bits. Our humor was long-winded enough for articles of a column or more. Ernest Thayer, '85, dignified in conversation by the title of Count, was prolific in them and indispensable to us. The bulk of the paper was sometimes by his hand. His aspect always had the soberness—I should say the seriousness—which goes with true wit: he observed everything ludicrous with a sleepy serenity, as if it were the time of day. His graduation left Lampy with only the '86 Board to rely on for proof, and the class tried to make up in quantity of editors what it was conscious of lacking in quality of wit. We had eight or ten members, which was then thought a large Board.

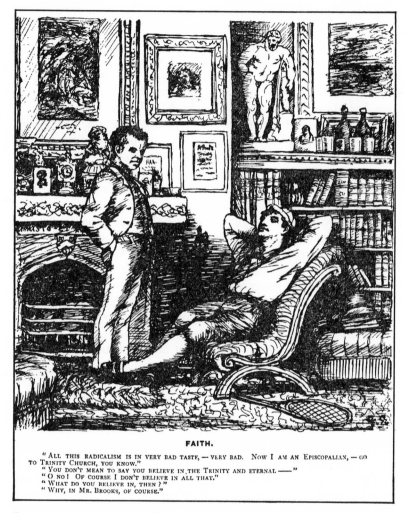

FAITH.

"ALL THIS RADICALISM IS IN VERY BAD TASTE, — VERY BAD. NOW I AM AN EPISCOPALIAN, — GO TO TRINITY CHURCH, YOU KNOW."

"YOU DON'T MEAN TO SAY YOU BELIEVE IN THE TRINITY AND ETERNAL ——"

"O NO! OF COURSE I DON'T BELIEVE IN ALL THAT."

"WHAT DO YOU BELIEVE IN, THEN?"

"WHY, IN MR. BROOKS, OF COURSE."

Santayana is referring to the Rev. Philips Brooks, who became rector of Trinity Church in 1869, the same year Charles W. Eliot became president of Harvard. Both men contributed greatly to cultural changes in New England. Santayana did this cartoon for the May 18, 1883, issue of the Lampoon.

The college world was then less diversified, and we could float through its nebulous masses without feeling at any time very far removed from its centre. We lived about the Yard. Beck and Little's were our Claverly and Randolph. There were only two clubs, and the classes had still a good deal of solidarity. Everybody knew what was going on and anybody could be intelligibly funny about it. A paper was not a public organization; it was a private amusement supported by advertising tradesmen. Nobody would have dreamt of confessing that he was "trying" for the *Lampoon,* any more than he would avow he was "trying" for the Porcellian. Trying and swiping, in that primitive stage of evolution, had not yet been differentiated. "Lampy," we might have said, "Lampy *c'est nous.*" Yet in his private capacity the Jester was a purely Harvard imp, disporting himself for the benefit of the college. Harvard itself did not yet mean an engine. It meant people.

The illustrations of our day were rather negligent. The neat and decorative style had died out with Nichols, and we were altogether vulgar and pre-aesthetic. Nor did we have any real caricature, such as earlier times had known. But if we accomplished little we had small pretensions. Even in those days, when subjects and ideas gave out, we had learned to appeal to the eternal idyl: a man and a girl for the picture, and for the words, anything. Memorial Hall soup and the puddles in the Yard gave a family likeness to every number, so that the reader, however startled by the novelties of the issue, could always reassure himself that Lampy was the same old Lampy still. May he long prosper, and amid his new glories keep something of his careless and unworldly youth, when he took "*Vanitas*" for a motto.

THOMAS PARKER SANBORN

By the death of Thomas Parker Sanborn of the class of '86, the MONTHLY loses one of its founders and first contributors. The rare facility and delicacy of Mr. Sanborn's verses, and his general literary aptitude, marked him out among his class-mates. His witty conversation, and much more the inward seriousness and idealism of his nature endeared him to those that knew him well. He was too sensitive and retiring to like general society, or to speak out his thoughts: he was more at ease with his pen. Besides being an editor of the MONTHLY, he was at one time editor of the *Advocate*, and also president of the *Lampoon*. After leaving college he continued to write. Some of his pieces have appeared in *Life*, and others in the *Springfield Republican*, of which he had become an assistant editor.

Mr. Sanborn had not only great felicity of style in his light verses: but he could put into them what is far more rare in the work of very young men,—a true love of whatever is charming, beautiful and ideal. His poetry was the real, if not the adequate, expression of his feeling; it was the channel by which he could

Santayana published this obituary on his friend in *The Harvard Monthly*, March, 1889. He and Sanborn had served together on the original board of editors.

escape from the sense of the imperfection, the aridity, of the commonplace world about him. He was haunted perpetually by a feeling of estrangement, of disparity, between himself and what he cared for on the one hand, and the external world and its ways on the other. Yet with this idealism was joined a genuine and pathetic modesty. He was afraid he was wrong, he longed for recognition and external encouragement. He suffered at the suspicion, often ungrounded, that he lacked the sympathy of others, and any mark of appreciation and liking gave him keen pleasure. It was not his vanity that was flattered, but his dread of isolation that was relieved. So sensitive and subjective a temper naturally tends to exaggerate its own peculiarity; and this tendency, added to a never vigorous health, led in the end to moments of extreme depression and of hallucination, in one of which he took his life.

This premature death is a calamity not to Mr. Sanborn's family and intimate friends alone. The class of '86 and Harvard College lose a man whose life would have been devoted to letters, and whose genuine and versatile talent would hardly have failed to leave some mark in the world.

A GLIMPSE OF YALE

The ideas which have most influence over our feelings are sometimes the vaguest and the phrases most often on our lips have the least definable meaning. Such, for the Harvard man, is the idea conveyed by the short word YALE. We know what emotion belongs to it, and if we were not afraid of wounding polite ears we might readily enough supply its appropriate context. If we attempted, however, to explain this irritation to a stranger, or to justify it to ourselves, we should soon be involved in difficulties. We feel that Yale is at once most similar and most opposite to Harvard, that she is not only a rival in those things, such as athletics, which are common to both colleges, but at the same time an embodiment of what is most hostile to our spirit. Yet this feeling, even if it should prove justifiable, is not generally grounded on any actual knowledge. It is a vague intuition which experience has never tested. If we knew Yale better, should we not feel all our mistrust dissolve and our coldness thaw? Should we not feel the substantial identity of our aims and history? Should we not marvel that mere rivalry in sport, which ought to be above all things good-natured and friendly, should have pro-

This essay appeared in *The Harvard Monthly*, December, 1892.

duced such an unnatural prejudice between two neighboring colleges?

The desire to verify this suspicion, as far as it could be verified in a two days' visit, carried me not long ago to New Haven. I should not venture to speak at all after such brief observation, had I not learned a few facts unknown perhaps to many readers of the MONTHLY, as they were hitherto unknown to me, and had not my own first impression of Yale surprised me by its strength and agreeableness.

New Haven is a pleasant town of nearly a hundred thousand inhabitants well situated between the Sound and harbor on the one side, and a range of hills upon the other, which rise in places to a precipitous grandeur. The streets are arched over with elms, and the houses in the better parts stand each on its own plot of ground and have a pleasing and sometimes a stately air. You feel that the inmates must be worthy people, all the nicer for not having thriven inordinately and gone to live in New York. The lawns are lovely, the flower-beds well kept; an instinct tells you that there is good housewifery within, and that the mother of the family is a gentle and delightful person. The college Campus is in the midst of the town, upon one side of the small common, or Green. It is much more closely built upon than our Yard. The structures are of different styles and periods, much as our own, but the incongruities are less glaring; the colors of the brick and stone melt into each other, and the packing of the buildings around small courts and spaces makes it impossible for any of them to stand out, like Matthews or Thayer in its hideous totality. In spite of the nearness of the streets and the comparative absence of verdure, there is an effect of retirement. The walls encircle you on every side and overlap one another. The earth is well trodden under foot, and crossed by many stretches of pavement; the due line of paths is not marked out, as with us, by six inches of newly laid grass and a stretched wire. The whole Campus has unmistakable suggestions of a true college quadrangle. The outlying buildings are less satisfactory. Osborne Hall distresses the eye with its confused pretentiousness, and the great new gymnasium, perhaps too intentionally grand, makes one ask whether an athlete or a monarch holds his court at the head of the marble stairs, and whether the *porte cochere* is meant to give passage to a chariot or to an ambulance.

The Yale Field, where the games are held and the running track is situated, lies a mile and a half away. To reach it you pass through a part of the town and through one of those outlying districts where empty lots gape on every side, new houses to let expose their blank walls, curbstones with an occasional lamp-post emerge from the sands, and ragged children play with rubbish. But soon you cross a bridge and the scene becomes more rural, a turn brings you to a gate, you ascend a slope, and your trouble is repaid by a delightful prospect. You are upon a level top of a wide plateau: low hills appear in the distance beyond the surrounding depressions. To the left is a comfortable little house, painted red, where the teams dress; beyond it a screen of beautiful trees is outlined against the sky. To the right is the grand stand. For the baseball season seats are built on either side of this, the wide sweep of the outfield being left free for carriages; but at foot-ball games the grand stand is not used and the custom is to stand or walk about the ropes. The crowd follows the game from one side to the other with keen and intelligent interest, as if each man felt that he was a possible substitute. A foot-ball game is always a fine spectacle, but here upon the broad backed earth, away from the town, nothing but sky and distant hills about you, where the wind always blows, the struggle has an added beauty. It borrows from the bleak and autumnal landscape something of a pathetic earnestness and natural horror. It seems to embody a primal instinct, to be a symbol of all the prehistoric struggles of our earth-born race. Here the heroic virtues shine in miniature, and the simple glory of the savage world returns as in a dream. The young men stand about, absorbed and admiring, commenting like the crowd in Homer upon the prowess of their chiefs. It is an unforgettable sight: but soon the run is made or the goal kicked, and as you look about with relaxed attention, you notice perhaps some smart carriage driving in with its bouquet of pretty faces peeping from their furs and violets, and this shrill note of fashion, with its possible overtones of love, relieves the rude intensity of the scene.

Here, at the Field, one comes upon the most crying expression of that Yale Spirit of which we hear so much: "hustle"—a contagion of energy, and "get there"—a reckless love of success. Those popular philosophers who have a fondness for finding spirits in things should not fail to visit Yale, for there their native talent for spirit-seeing would be exercised on the most favorable object. No contemplation of nature, no reading of history, could suggest more powerfully to their minds the presence of a pervasive metaphysical power, some disembodied energy brooding over the incidents of life and controlling them. If we were not born

> Too late for antique vows,
> Too, too late for the fond believing lyre,

we might yet build an altar to the Yale Spirit upon Jarvis Field, as the Israelites did to Baal upon Mount Zion, and beseech that terrible divinity with many hymns to take us also under its protection. But since we are grown too unimaginative for such genial superstitions, we must be satisfied with studying the body of this Spirit, and with trying to discover the mechanism by which it moves its arms and legs in such startling and miraculous concert.

The first ingredient of the Yale Spirit is of course the raw material of the students. They come, as is well known, from many parts of the country, and this diversity of origin and associations would seem at first sight to be an obstacle to unity. But it is not. Each boy in his distant high school or academy has been looking forward to the day when he should find himself in the great college; this has been the dream of his boyhood. When he arrives he comes upon entirely strange scenes, where he is dependent for all his pleasures and successes on his ability to make new friends and to play an indispensable part in the undergraduate world. The traditions of the place become sacred to him and he vies with his fellow students in proving that he understands them. His family and early friends are far away. The new influences soon control him entirely and imprint upon his mind and manner the unmistakable mark of his college. College ideals are for the time being his only ideals, college successes the only successes. The Yale man is not often such by halves or incidentally; he does not so often as the Harvard man retain an underlying allegiance to the social and intellectual standards of his family, by virtue of which he allows himself to criticise and perhaps to despise the college hero. Divisions of wealth and breeding are not made conspicuous at Yale as at Harvard by the neighborhood of a city with well-marked social sets, the most fashionable of which sends all its boys to the college. These boys—so much does extreme youth prevail among us—form the most conspicuous masculine contingent of Boston society, and the necessity falls upon them of determining which of their college friends are socially presentable. This circumstance brings out at Harvard an element of snobbery which at Yale is in abeyance. The college hero is there most unreservedly admired, and although it is not true that the most coveted societies are open to everyone who gains distinction in scholarship or athletics, other considerations have relatively much less weight than among us. The relations of one Yale student to another are comparatively simple and direct. They are like passengers in a ship or fellow countrymen abroad; their sense of common interests and common emotions overwhelms all latent antipathies. They live in a sort of primitive brotherhood, with a ready enthusiasm for every good or bad project, and a contagious good-humor.

Another cause combines with isolation from the outer world and internal homogeneity to give vigor to the Yale Spirit. It is college discipline. Every morning you must be at chapel at ten minutes past eight; at half-past eight everybody has a recitation. All the work of the Freshman and Sophomore years is prescribed; you sit with the same men and all your class has the same tasks and the same teachers. There is a regular tariff of black marks for offences of negligence, so many for tardiness at chapel, so many for absence, so many if you cut more than six lectures in a course, so many if you cut successive lectures, and most of all—eight marks—if you are absent from church on Sunday. When twenty marks are received a letter is written to your father; forty-eight marks in one term involve suspension, unless the ruling powers can be mollified, as they perhaps might be by a good athletic record.* The habit of doing things together is thus formed at Yale, and concerted action of all kinds is easy there. There is more noise and bustle in the Campus than in our Yard. If a fire alarm sounds, every student flings open his window, pops his head out, and yells, "Fire" for all he is worth. The unpopular proctor's windows are not safe from stones, nor even his door

---

* A Yale professor once told me that, although the faculty as a body was not particularly lenient to athletics, it was well understood that the various instructors were so in their individual capacity. [Santayana's note.]

from a battering ram. Unhappy the lecturer whom any singular-
ity of voice or manner exposes to the ridicule of his class! nor will
a dull speaker retain his pupils if they find a door, a window, or a
fire-escape at hand. These are school-boy tricks that go with
compulsory lessons, but they lend a certain quaint humor to
college life and are delightful to remember. They have also a
social function. Common grievances are a greater bond than
common privileges, and the chapel bell, the system of marks, the
prescribed mathematics, and the unpopular instructor are so
many forces that make for union in the undergraduate world.

In fact, Yale is in many respects what Harvard used to be. It
has maintained the traditions of a New England college more
faithfully. Anyone visiting the two colleges would think Yale by
far the older institution. The past of America makes itself felt
there in many subtle ways: there is a kind of colonial self-
reliance, and simplicity of aim, a touch of non-conformist separation from the great ideas and movements of the world. One is
reminded, as one no longer is at Harvard, of Burke's phrase
about the dissidence of dissent and the Protestantism of the
Protestant religion. Nor is it only the past of America that is
enshrined at Yale; the present is vividly portrayed there also.
Nothing could be more American—not to say *Amurrcan*—than
Yale College. The place is sacred to the national ideal. Here is
sound, healthy principle, but no overscrupulousness, love of life,
trust in success, a ready jocoseness, a democratic amiability, and
a radiant conviction that there is nothing better than one's self. It
is a boyish type of character, earnest and quick in things practical, hasty and frivolous in things intellectual. But the boyish ideal
is a healthy one, and in a young man, as in a young nation, it is
perfection to have only the faults of youth. There is sometimes
a beautiful simplicity and completeness in the type which this
ideal produces. One of the most impressive things I saw at Yale
was the room officially occupied by the secretary of the Young
Men's Christian Association. It was a pretty room, the windows
high in the wall, as a student's windows should be. There were
books and teacups and a pot of white chrysanthemums in bloom.
The stove alone might have disfigured the place, but it was
covered by a heap of foot-balls, battered and dirty, each with the
word Harvard or Princeton painted upon it. They were trophies

which a former secretary of the association and captain of the foot-ball team had brought to this sanctum from the field. It is delightful to see this full-hearted wholeness, this apparently perfect adjustment between man and his environment, this buoyant faith in one's divine mission to be rich and happy. No wonder that all America loves Yale, where American traditions are vigorous, American instincts are unchecked, and young men are trained and made eager for the keen struggles of American life.

I have mentioned the word religion. It is there that we touch the vital and fundamental point. Yale has a religion. The solution of the greatest problems is not sought, it is regarded as already discovered. The work of education is to instil these revealed principles and to form habits congruous with them. Everything is arranged to produce a certain type of man. The scope of study, it is true, is becoming very wide, and a glance at the programme of courses would not suggest much more bias in the instruction than there is at Harvard or at a German university. But in reality these miscellaneous studies are at Yale merely incidental; they are "frills," concessions to the foreign idea, to the new desire of being a university and of leaving nothing out. The essential object of the institution is still to educate rather than to instruct, to be a mother of men rather than a school of doctors. In this Yale has been true to the English tradition, and is, in fact, to America what Oxford and Cambridge are to England, a place where the tradition of national character is maintained, together with a traditional learning. If there is a difference, as of course there is, between the Yale undertone of crudity and toughness and the sweet mellowness of studious and athletic life in England, that is not the fault of Yale, but is due to the fact that English and American society are at different intellectual stages. The Yale principle is the English principle, and the only right one. As American society approaches maturity, and all human interests gain representation in it, a college like Yale will gradually ripen too. Its curriculum will be extended, its outlook will be widened, and its barbarism will disappear; but the initial intention and function will remain. The continuity with the past will not be broken, and the sympathy with the national life will never be lost. Whatever investigations the professors may incidentally carry on, their chief business will be to be the masters of their pupils, not merely to employ them as instruments for some problematic discovery of their own, but to transmit the enriched treasure of human experience to the generations that

Quasi cursores vitai lampada tradunt.[1]

If Harvard, in seeking after new gods, should forget this traditional and primary duty, she would surrender the moral leadership of the country which in the past, when she was a college like Yale, she undoubtedly had. There is, indeed, a very different ideal of a university. Our function might be to be a collection of museums, laboratories, and special libraries, to which everybody, when his professional work required it, might go for information. We might be used as people use the British Museum. And we might even add to this utility that which the German universities have. At the head of these laboratories, museums, and libraries there might be distinguished specialists, and students in their various branches might repair to them, attracted by their reputation or fascinated by their doctrine. This was the nature of mediaeval universities, and in Germany this type has never been superseded. The professor is there the power, not the institution, and the student wanders from place to place to hear all the famous teachers of the day. He is all the more willing to do so if he can leave his creditors behind him, and if he finds the beer as good and the girls as facile in one town as in another. To return to this type would be a retrogression, nor do I think that the Anglo-Saxon ideal of education, in which the aim is the formation of character and of taste, will be abandoned in this country. Harvard herself has no intention of abandoning it. If some people, eager to enlarge the scope of the university, have lost sight of it for the moment, they will soon be reminded of it by the demands of the public and by their own sense of the relative values of things. If Harvard errs, it is not in principle but in judgment. She may have too great a confidence in the public, too high an idea of what the times will bear. She thinks she may trust the earlier training and the social ties of her students to give a right direction to their lives and to inspire them with a consciousness of the true object of education. She therefore leaves it to

---

[1] "like runners hand on the torch of life." From Lucretius, *Of the Nature of Things*, Book II, line 75.

them to choose their studies and to form their interests. Her ideal aim is to offer every opportunity that any nature can require for its perfect cultivation. She therefore has no protective tariff on ideas; she believes that an impartial and scholarly survey of all the riches of nature and of history must make for good, morally as well as intellectually. This is her trust in truth, her motto *Veritas.*

Truth is also the motto of Yale, but with light preceding, *Lux et veritas,* as if at Yale they loved the truth because they believed they saw it clearly, while we love it even if it be wrapped in darkness. For Harvard also has a religion, although it is less obvious and articulate than that of Yale. I do not mean merely that we have here our Young Men's Christian Association, our chapel, our charities, our Divinity School, and our Christian philosophers. We have all these things, as with our generous conception of a university it is right and natural that we should have them. No one, however earnest in his faith, need be afraid of isolation among us. But beneath these specifically religious forces and permeating the whole community there is, I think, a vaguer but deeper religion—the faith in enlightenment, the aspiration to be just, the sympathy with the multiform thoughts and labors of humanity. This is surely the noblest inspiration, and one which unites us to all ages and places in which men have cultivated reason. No one, I am sure, who has felt this high passion and freely fostered it in these halls, will put any place above Harvard in his affection. Some universities have greater beauty and a richer past, some have maturer scholars and more famous teachers. Yale herself has more unity, more energy, and greater fitness to our present conditions. Harvard, instead of all these advantages, has freedom, both from external trammels and from the pleasant torpor of too fixed a tradition. She has freedom and a single eye for the truth, and these are enough to secure for her, if the world goes well, an incomparable future.

THE SPIRIT AND IDEALS OF HARVARD UNIVERSITY

When the visitor to the educational department of the Chicago Exhibition entered the section assigned to Harvard, the first thing that met his eyes was a case containing preparations of condensed milk for infants. The suspicion might come over him that he had mistaken the place—or could this be some covert allusion to the courses of study? A little beyond he found a collection of artificial arms and legs, and was the more bewildered, while visions of football and its dangers passed across his mind. Farther still he saw a series of views of solar eclipses. In one corner he then discovered—not the groups of the crew, the nine, and the eleven, which he was perhaps looking for—but at least an equivalent in the chart of physical development and the photographs of naked athletes. Finally he entered a darkened and academic chamber where portraits of ancient worthies, works of distinguished alumni, and other trophies of the national glory of Harvard were gathered together. Here he received from the hands of an attendant various pamphlets, which, if he stopped to read them, gave him some idea of the extent and variety of the learning pursued at Cambridge. He would then find it possible to

This essay appeared in *The Educational Review*, April, 1894.

explain the strange impression which his first entrance produced. He would understand that he had happened to come in by the corner assigned to the medical school. He would also understand that photography of the heavens is a specialty of the astronomical observatory. He would see that if a certain incapacity to win from Yale seems to beset Harvard athletic teams, this is not due to any official neglect or discouragement of physical training, or to any inferiority in the young men individually. And if he was prepared by adequate knowledge or instinctive comprehension, he would feel also that a sense of the stability and dignity of the institution carried with it a reluctance to push forward the individuality of its living members and a willingness to be satisfied with recalling the names of a few of its distinguished dead. He would, in brief, carry away the conviction that Harvard was scientific, that it was complex, and that it was reserved.

In these three words I should be tempted to sum up all that can be made articulate in the present spirit and ideals of Harvard. There is hardly here any commanding thought or specific mission such as can inspire a denominational or technical institution. Some colleges have a spirit and ideal in the sense that they are founded for a single and definite purpose which directs all their life from above. Such a spirit is a conscious and explicit ideal, and the establishment is its intentional manifestation. Harvard is not the instrument of such a design. In the beginning it may have been so, but the ancient object of training a pious and learned clergy has long since dropped out of sight. After being Unitarian for a while the divinity school has become neutral, and is not a large or conspicuous part of the university. The teaching there is guided by the same scientific spirit that is conspicuous everywhere else at Harvard; it is the truth that is taught, but the truth without a capital letter. The lapse of the primitive function of the college has not given place to any other single overruling aim. The kind of spirit, therefore, which I can describe is only the resultant of many individual inspirations. I cannot point to a sovereign organizing force, I can only describe certain widespread characteristics.

Of these characteristics the most notable is scientific enthusiasm and liberty of thought. The growth of the community and of the college in wealth and numbers has made an increasing force of professors and instructors necessary. These men, gener-

ally students of high standing who after graduation have seen
something of German universities, cannot conceive their function
as did the worthy teacher of a hundred years ago, whose ambition was, while gaining heaven for himself, to infuse Euclid and
virtue into the souls of his pupils. Some teachers of the old school
naturally remain—teachers in whom the moral and personal relation to their pupils is still predominant, but the main concern of
our typical young professor is not his pupils at all. It is his
science. His vocation is to follow and promote the development
of his branch of learning by reading the new books and magazine
articles on his subject and contributing himself to its "literature."
He gives lectures and reads his students' theses, and often, no
doubt, finds this a welcome labor. There are times when light and
inspiration come to him in the process of sifting and communicat-
ing his knowledge, times when he takes a natural delight in
expressing his ideas—which he is here so free to do—and in
planting the seeds of scholarship in the rising generation. But,
generally speaking, he wishes to be a scholar, and is a teacher
only by accident, only because scholars are as yet supported only
by institutions whose primary object is the education of youth.
The pupils whom he really welcomes are those who have chosen
his own profession and can encourage him in his labors by their
sympathy and collaboration. His real colleagues also are not so
much the other professors at the university as his *Fachgenossen*
all the world over. His moments of genuine expansion, of true
intellectual fellowship, come when he meets some one of these
fellow-laborers; then some profound discussion, relieved by the
news and gossip of the science, may keep him up until the small
hours, in rare forgetfulness of the next morning's early recitation.

The method of instruction has become scientific no less than
the inspiration of the teacher. The subjects are distributed into
separate groups, each of which has professors, assistant professors, and instructors exclusively belonging to it, and forming a
committee or sub-faculty which practically decides all questions
of instruction and honors in its province. In every department the
effort is made to cover the ground in a systematic fashion, so that
no important part of its material, historical or scientific, shall be
absent from the curriculum. Considering the poverty of the university and the consequently limited number of professors, this
has been done with remarkable success, and Harvard may boast

that it is, in the literal sense, a university. This feat involves, however, an undesirable lack of freedom on the teacher's part in the selection of his subjects, since his courses must fill in the gaps of the programme of the department, nor is it yet the custom for an instructor to offer courses already given by another. A more adequate endowment would naturally make these obstacles disappear.

Another direction in which methodical instruction has advanced may be illustrated by the organization of the English department. This division, besides giving courses in the history of English literature, undertakes to drill the younger students in the use of their mother-tongue, and to piece out the shocking deficiencies of their previous education in this particular. Twenty teachers are enrolled in this department. There is an elaborate organism of courses, some prescribed for more or less advanced students, others elective. The machinery of handing in "briefs" and "forensics," "themes" and compositions of various sorts at stated times and places; their correction in hieroglyphics to which the department publishes an official key, and their return to the students for correction or rewriting—all the elaborate discipline of the department makes one think of a post-office, or of the mechanism of some great business bureau. This ungrateful but perhaps necessary task is carried through in a very wide-awake and efficient manner, and while the teachers in it are generally much overworked and need to exercise extraordinary patience to read attentively so much incoherent and careless writing, the students seem to take the thing in good part, and to grumble less than they might be expected to do at the only study which is still compulsory for them.

For the growth of scientific devotion in the professors has brought about corresponding changes in the scope of instruction and in the discipline of the college. To teach the outworn formulae of a science when new and interesting developments were absorbing the teacher's mind was no longer possible or honest. The best must be given, and the variety and profusion of modern scholarship must find some expression in the courses of instruction. At the same time it was obviously impossible for a student to absorb all the learning of fifty professors; a selection of courses became necessary, and a problem arose about the method of this selection. The "group system" would naturally suggest itself; but it would require the determination of certain ideals of learning. Thus at Oxford, the *litterae humaniores* are regarded as the proper prescription for a man of literary and philosophic tastes. But at Harvard the alternative studies allowed at first had been single courses, which a student might add to his prescribed studies; gradually the number of these optional courses increased, and the prescribed curriculum was restricted to make room for the "electives." Consequently the expansion of the university took place, not by the multiplication of curricula between which, as wholes, the students might choose, but by the abandonment of a stated curriculum altogether, and the opening of the entire list of courses to each student. This is the well-known elective system, which has had far-reaching results both in the scholarship and the morale of the college.

It was nearly ten years ago, when freshman work and chapel were successively made elective, that this system reached its full development here. It was accompanied by, and partly founded upon, the theory that all real work, all work worthy of a university man, should be spontaneous; that it was the student's own business to make his college life profitable; that the university must merely give him the opportunity. It was the ideal long before invoked by Emerson, who wished attendance at lectures to be voluntary, and the control of the students' conduct to be in the hands of the ordinary city police. Athletics were not then regulated and restrained by committees of the faculty. Perhaps this fact was due to the comparative absence of the athletic spirit in those days, when the present enthusiasm on that subject, somewhat artificial here, had not been stirred up by contagion from other colleges. At the same time the reigning feeling was that if a youth passed his examinations and conformed to the other official requirements, it was nobody's business how he spent his time or broke his bones. A student might then make a trip to Cuba or Florida in term time without serious consequences; and I remember that as a sophomore I cut all but two recitations in a course that met once a week throughout the year, and passed by merely taking the examinations, without any warning or sign of disapproval from the authorities. This was in 1884; soon after there set in a strong reaction. The public and the overseers became alarmed at the neglect with which the students were favored, and urged stricter supervision and guidance. Their feeling found more or less response in the faculty itself, and now, although the elective system remains, a very different spirit inspires the college government. When a freshman comes to Cambridge he is assigned to an adviser—popularly called his nurse—who supervises his proposed list of studies, and attempts to make his personal acquaintance and to exercise some influence over his walk and conversation. Throughout the course the student is required to be assiduous at recitations; unannounced examinations, frequent written questions, and all other means that are found practicable, help to keep him at his daily work. There is a good deal of dropping and sending away of lazy youths. All are compelled to report on the morning after vacation, no absence from Cambridge during term time is allowed without good excuse, and the athletic and other organizations of the college are watched with a jealous, although generally benevolent, eye. The result is a very noticeable air of diligence in the place; there is more general interest in work, and everyone seems busier than in the old days. The system of special reports and frequent theses which has grown up has contributed greatly to this improvement; for it keeps the students at their books, sends them to the library for references, and maintains the sense of an impending test more vividly than could be done by semi-annual examinations alone. Whether the final effect is better, especially in the case of intelligent students, and whether the reaction against the more liberal system is to be permanent, are further questions which we need not discuss. There are not wanting in the faculty persons convinced that a system of perfect freedom, friendly confidence, and responsibility to self is alone proper for higher instruction and for the moral development of young men. Such a free system practically exists in the graduate schools, where the age and earnestness of the majority of the students make it appropriate; but the bad discipline of preparatory schools and the absence of strong intellectual and social traditions at the university seem to make it unsafe for undergraduates at present. It would leave the freshman, coming to Cambridge for the first time, too much isolated and in too great danger of wasting his opportunities.

If the present situation had been foreseen when the college began to expand into a university, the graduate school might simply have been added to the old academic department, and allowed to grow and become a nursery of all the sciences without the restraints of discipline, while the college might have retained all the strength of its traditions and its essential function of educating the taste and character of youths. It is now too late to establish this dualism, although a certain tendency in that direction is visible in the highest quarters. The obstacle that stands in the way is the fact that the college has already got beyond the phase at which it ought to have stopped if it was to have realized this ideal. The elective system and the opening of advanced and technical courses to undergraduates has raised it to the level of a university, carrying it essentially beyond the sphere of the *Gymnasium,* the *Lycée,* or the Jesuit College, which have the function suggested for it in this plan. The college and the graduate school are therefore essentially similar and continuous, and Harvard is, more or less unconsciously, trying an interesting experiment, which if successful should give it a very eminent position indeed among all institutions of learning. This experiment consists in the attempt to raise an old-fashioned American college to the level of scholarship, freedom, and decorum which should characterize graduate studies, and at the same time to retain in it, and infuse into a graduate school gathered around it, the corporate traditions, the social life, and the unity of feeling which make the vitality and educational power of the college.

For it is Harvard College that has a history and enlists the sympathies of the community; it alone has a spiritual existence and touches the hearts and the pockets of the great body of alumni. To Harvard College they wish to send their sons, to have them afterward follow some profession or a mercantile life, having first got there the education of a gentleman. To Harvard College belong the social and athletic traditions of the place, without which, of course, there would be no essential difference between Harvard and Clark University. Wherever one may afterward go to study—and it makes little difference where when one is old enough to teach oneself—it is in Harvard College that one has lived and been educated—and that makes a difference throughout one's life. The Harvard graduate school is useful and excellent; as a place of study I should not hesitate, to judge from my own experience, to prefer it to those German universities to which American students flock in search of the last words of science. The number of professors is not so great, perhaps, but their quality is not inferior, and the facilities for study in the way of books and personal direction are much greater. But with all its merits the graduate school has necessarily no intellectual, moral, or social unity. The majority of the students are forlorn atoms, and their concourse is too fortuitous ever to make a world. It is impossible to have any affection or loyalty for such an aggregation, however excellent the instruction supplied to its constituent parts. The traditional support given to Harvard College cannot pass to the graduate school for the simple reason that a man who has been only at the graduate school is not a Harvard man.

What has been said will already have given some suggestion of the complexity of the university. The divinity school, the law school, and the graduate school are at Cambridge locally fused with the college. They contain many Harvard graduates who, while they remain in their old haunts, naturally keep up the traditions and associations of their college life. At Cambridge also is the rapidly growing scientific school, which has a prescribed curriculum according to the group system, and is separated from the college by the different character and aims of the students. In Boston is the medical school, which has little connection with the rest of the university, except that many of its professors and students are Harvard graduates. The same may be said of the smaller appendages to the college—the Bussey Institute of Agriculture, the botanical garden, and the dental and veterinary schools. The astronomical observatory is a more dignified but not less isolated institution. The professors of the various faculties seldom meet and often do not know one another by sight. The only connection among these departments is through the persons of the president and fellows, who control their finances and to a great extent their policy. When one attempts to survey at a glance so great a number and variety of activities, all within the pale of one institution, one has very much that sense of hopeless intricacy and wonder at the smooth running of the whole which is produced by the inspection of a great factory or by the description of a great government. It is a very large machine serving the needs of a very complex civilization.

After noting this external many-sidedness of Harvard and its manifold aims, we shall be helped to complete our impression if we glance at the students' life and see the diversity of pursuits and ideals there. The diversity is indeed so great, and the individuality of the students so marked, that all classifications and descriptions of types are apt to be misleading. One-half the students must be conceived as very poor, brought to college by intellectual and practical ambition, working hard at their books and for their maintenance, and without time or money for much recreation, exercise, or society. This class, from which the best scholars generally come, is dubbed "the grinds," and although so numerous and important, passes unnoticed by the public, and by its lack of association is not a force even in college life. The official honors which often fall to its members are unfortunately not much valued at Harvard. Although the worthy student of this class is personally respected by all, he is known to very few and gets no popular recognition. No less unobserved and solitary is another sort of student, often a rich and sometimes an interesting one—the man whose interests and associations are all beyond college life. He is apt to be an eccentric person, who despises or affects to despise what others care about, and made unpopular at first by something in his manner, birth, or appearance, revenges himself on the college world by holding aloof from it. He and the "grind," although the least known and counted, are perhaps the most truly characteristic of Harvard types.

These solitaries apart, there are three centers around which college life gathers—the athletic teams, the papers and literary societies, and the clubs. The first two have not at Harvard that spontaneous support which seems to sustain the corresponding things in other colleges. There must be athletic teams, there must be papers, there must be literary societies; they have existed hitherto, and it devolves on each successive class to take them up and do the best it can with them. Supported by this sense of duty, they lead a laborious existence. Some of the best athletes complain in private of the pressure that keeps them training and playing. There is here little of Spartan unanimity and unquestioning zeal. There is criticism and self-consciousness instead. Debating societies, for instance, once so vigorous, and everywhere so characteristic of the Anglo-Saxon temper, languish at Harvard, and exist by the efforts of a few amid the indifference or blushes of the many. To talk in public for the sake of talking seems here a little like foolish loudness. Even social bodies—Greek-letter societies, for instance—change their character at

Harvard. The chapters of two of the most influential of them have seceded from their respective fraternities and become purely local clubs, and the others are practically as independent. Only one important society retains a secret and elaborate initiation; it meets with much opposition on that account, and has once or twice been on the point of extinction; but it has been revived, because by no other means could men of successive classes get to know one another intimately, or the smaller clubs be intelligently recruited. These smaller clubs have no exercises or meetings, except occasional dinners; they are very private, but in no sense secret, and are run exactly like town clubs, with a restaurant included. Life in them has nothing particularly collegiate about it, but is very pleasant and orderly, and naturally the basis of many warm friendships.

This complex social organization—which the undergraduate takes very seriously—explains a good deal of that reserve and exclusiveness, that non-conductiveness and apathy, which is noticeable in the typical Harvard man. But there are many other factors in this general characteristic. The elective system has done its share. It has broken up the classes, the only natural unities in so great a mass of students; it has thrown each man back on himself and on his personal friends; it has developed his individuality, his judgment, and his habit of relying on himself. It has, by habitual isolation, hardened him against the contagion both of good and evil. For it is a truth which must not go unnoticed that this reserve does not mean only lack of enthusiasm, it means also strength and self-respect. I doubt very much that anywhere in the world there could be found three thousand young men, many of them with plenty of time and money to spare, living away from home near a large city, who show such a general average of virtue, so much steady self-restraint, such a habitual and constitutional choice of the nobler thing in conduct and in feeling. Of course there are some wild fellows, there are many who have, in one direction or another, occasional lapses from grace; but the tone is healthy and sensible, and honor and welcome always go out to the better nature. Athletic training—of which with all the 'varsity and class teams there is a good deal—accustoms everyone to see, if not to practice, the utmost strictness; and a man may refuse to drink and smoke even in the freest circles without encountering troublesome protests. And it is not only moral independence and worth that we find here: we find very generally a certain mental maturity and balance. This is another virtue which underlies "Harvard indifference." What seems coldness is often justice, and tardiness of enthusiasm often comes from mental perspective and a steady sense of what is ideally best. It is easy to be full of zeal and bluster, to cheer and push on any enterprise, however flimsy, and applaud any loud orator, however inapt, if one knows or cares nothing about what is essentially reasonable and fine. The community from which Harvard men are chiefly drawn is not of the crudest, and the spirit in which they are educated is free and catholic; they have often, therefore, a sense of proportion, a sense of the other possibility and of the better thing beyond, which may make them seem to dally and not to throw their whole soul into the things they do.

The air of reserve which is characteristic of Harvard has another, perhaps deeper, source. The constant and many-sided progression of everything here, the diligent labor of so many persons, the transformation of so many thoughts and things— where does it all lead? We do not know. We hope and believe vaguely that it is all a great work, and will have, and has hourly, its abundant reward. But this reward is not easy to see; no one can authoritatively point to it and tell us what it is. We lack the unity of a definite faith, we look to the future to enlighten us on the most fundamental questions. Each man knows the value of his own work and is sure that in itself it is worth doing if only for its immediate result in himself and in his pupils; but he feels also the relativity of this work and of its value without being able to survey the whole organism of human interests and adjust himself confidently to the universal life. All is tentative, and the goal, the final truth, is not clearly seen. This sense that we are experimenting, exploring, that our efforts are partial, imperfect, and partly, perhaps, in the wrong direction, and that the totality of our minds is a chaos—this sense is what imposes upon us an attitude of expectancy, or reserve. And by this industry in doubt while Harvard loses in a kind of brutal efficiency it catches the spirit of the age and worthily represents both its successes and its problems.

Part II

EMERSON AND WHITMAN

Editor's note: Santayana had a liking for Emerson and Whitman: the one, for his ability to rise above present concerns, even transcendentalism, and contemplate the world from the vantage of an original mind; the other, for his aggressiveness toward the genteel tradition in American letters. In both we see Santayana praising elements which are attitudes he himself has taken. But though he admired their originality of expression and their vital energy in an America desperately needing new voices, he remained suspicious of Emerson's escape into mysticism and of Whitman's desire to remain a "barbarian."

The two essays on Emerson supplement the well-known essay appearing in *Interpretations of Poetry and Religion* and remarks on Emerson made in "The Genteel Tradition in American Philosophy." Those essays treat mainly of Emerson's character, a subject, Santayana says in "The Optimism of Ralph Waldo Emerson," which reveals most about Emerson's vision. Thus, "The Optimism of Ralph Waldo Emerson" and "Emerson's Poems Proclaim the Divinity of Nature" serve to complete Santayana's treatment of Emerson by dealing specifically with Emerson's essays and poetry respectively.

In some ways the *jeu d'esprit* "Walt Whitman: A Dialogue" is a more revealing comment than the better-known remarks on

Whitman in "The Poetry of Barbarism" in *Interpretations of Poetry and Religion.* In "Walt Whitman: A Dialogue" Santayana is not as condemnatory of Whitman's barbaric impulses, and he leads the way to later remarks, as in "The Genteel Tradition in American Philosophy" and *Character and Opinion in the United States,* where he talks of Whitman's contribution to the dissolution of the genteel tradition. But Santayana also reveals his own comprehensive mind here as McStout, the classicist, and Van Tender, the romanticist, argue the virtues of Whitman's poetry. Although Santayana's own classical position in poetry allows McStout to have the last word, his naturalism causes Van Tender's arguments to be convincing. Santayana shows that he admired Whitman's naturalism; but he also attributes Whitman's ultimate failure to contribute to American culture to his lack of form.

THE OPTIMISM OF RALPH WALDO EMERSON

I

When the worth of life is called in question, as it frequently is nowadays, some amiable people grow impatient. They assure us that our troubles are merely interruptions of a natural state of happiness, that life on the whole is pleasant; and this cheerful dictum passes among them for optimism. The optimism of Emerson is of a different sort. He may sometimes grow impatient of the cynics and pessimists; but he does not answer them by a misstatement of the facts of experience. He does not attempt to compare the amounts of pain and pleasure in the world; perhaps he thought such a comparison impossible, perhaps he feared it might prove discouraging, or perhaps he saw that it would have little significance. For even if we were sure that the total of pleasure in the world was greater than the total of pain, what meaning would there be in calling such a world happy? We do

---

Under the pseudonym "Victor Cousin," Santayana submitted this essay for the 1886 Bowdoin Prize competition. He was not successful. This essay is published here from the original manuscript. Brackets are used to include material omitted from Emerson's prose or to clarify the reading. The essay has been edited previously with a brief introduction by Maurice F. Brown in the *Emerson Society Quarterly*, No. 37, 1964.

not call a voyage happy because less than half the crew has been lost.

At any rate, Emerson's philosophy is raised so far above these calculations that, champion of cheerfulness as he is, he does not hesitate to surrender the field of experience to the weeping philosophers. "Each man sees his own life defaced and disfigured. . . . Let any man go back to those delicious relations which have given him sincerest instruction and nourishment, he will shrink and moan. Alas! I know not why, infinite compunctions embitter in mature life the remembrances of budding joy, and cover every beloved name. Everything is beautiful seen from the point of view of intellect, or as truth. But all is sour, if seen as experience. . . . In the actual world, the painful kingdom of time and place, dwell care, and canker, and fear. With thought, with the ideal, is immortal hilarity, the rose of joy. Round it all the Muses sing. But grief clings to names, and persons, and the partial interests of today and yesterday."

In this passage Emerson already points out one main ground of his optimism, the world as idea, or as truth. But if we should pass immediately to the discussion of this conception, we might seem to beg the very question we are considering, namely, optimism. It cannot be denied that we should be following Emerson's example; for, after admitting some great evil in experience, he is too apt to bid us rejoice in the same thing as truth, without giving us time or reason to comfort ourselves for that evil experience. This abruptness and incompleteness may be pardoned in a poet; if his thought takes a sudden flight, his pen cannot stop to smooth the reader's way with explanations. We must follow if we can; if not, we must be content to wonder. But our present business is not merely to follow; it is to describe the journey; and we must do what we can to account for all its stages.

What consolation, then, does Emerson offer us for the evils of experience? Experience, after all, is what most of us care about; it is much more real to us than abstract truth; and that optimism would be far from reassuring which should ask us to welcome the doubts and sufferings of this life, because from the point of view of the intellect and as truth, the world is beautiful. We seek in experience its own justification; we expect optimism to show us that, within the field of experience, partial evil is universal good. This is what Leibnitz attempts to show; he teaches that every

event has its justification in history, and that if any evil had been
suppressed, a greater would necessarily have been introduced.
Suggestions of this doctrine are not wanting in Emerson. "The
first lesson of history[,]" he tells us, "is the good of evil. Good is a
good doctor, but Bad is sometimes a better. . . . Without war,
no soldier[s]; without enemies, no hero. . . . What would
painter do, or what would poet or saint, but for crucifixions and
hells?" But the title under which these remarks appear is for once
appropriate; they are only "considerations by the way." To give
these views a fundamental importance would be to misunderstand Emerson; his optimism consists in seeing that the world is
good, that it is very good; but not, like the optimism of Leibnitz,
in maintaining that it is the best world possible. These two
doctrines by no means involve each other. No serious philosopher
will deny that the evil in the world is necessary to bring about
the particular good in it; the pessimist is as ready as the optimist
to maintain that remotest events condition one another, and that
no part of the world could be changed without affecting the
whole. What is peculiar to Leibnitz is the doctrine that no better
series of events than the actual is possible; for, says he, if God had
had a better world to make, he would have made it; an argument
which may be used to prove, not that this world is good, but that
a good world is impossible. This suspicious theology does not
enter into Emerson's thought. He merely points out how the good
and evil of our lives grow out of each other; he shows them to be
inseparable. Far from making the evil disappear, he teaches that
it is the foundation of the good; we must expect evil and be
armed against it. It is not a wanton infliction; it comes in the
natural and necessary order of things. If we did not die, there
would be no room for our grandchildren; if we were never sick,
the amiable profession of medicine would be unknown. There
would be some effrontery in offering this consolation to a dying
man or to a cripple; but it comforts those of us who are young
and well.

Compensation, however, is an imposing law; and as teaching
the fear of the Lord, it may claim to be the beginning of wisdom.
Emerson likes to dwell on its curious rather than on its terrible
aspects; but he does not hesitate to draw from it the lesson of
indifference to circumstances. "Every sweet has its sour, every
evil its good." "There is a crack in everything God has made."

"He who by force of will or of thought is great and overlooks
thousands, has the charges of that eminence. With every influx of
light comes new danger. . . . He must hate father and mother,
wife and child. Has he all that the world [loves and] admires and
covets?—he must cast behind him their admiration, and afflict
them by faithfulness to his truth, and become a byword and a
hissing." One unmixed good he does present to us; but he finds it
out of experience, in "the aboriginal abyss of real Being." For
virtue, or quantity of being, we pay no tax; but all else is
compensated, all else is indifferent. From optimism of this kind,
pessimism differs only in name.

If Emerson does not take refuge in the doubtful satisfaction of
thinking no better world possible, much less does he console
himself with the hope of a pleasanter future. It is not strange that
he should have refused to speak as if suffering would be explained and justified the moment it should cease; this method of
silencing pain with the promise of sugar-plums is surely an
appeal to the irrational part of our nature. Emerson condemns it
with unusual vehemence. He has heard a sermon, in which the
doctrine of future rewards was unfolded in the ordinary manner,
and he asks: "What did the preacher mean by saying that the
good are miserable in the present life? Was it that houses and
lands, offices, wine, horses, [dress,] luxury, are had by unprinci-
pled men, whilst the saints are poor and despised; and that a
compensation is to be made to these [last] hereafter, by giving
them the like gratifications another day,—band-stock and doub-
loons, venison and champagne? This must be the compensation
intended; for what else? Is it that they are to have leave to pray
and praise? to love and serve men? Why, that they can do now.
The legitimate inference the disciple would draw was,—'We are
to have *such* a good time as the sinners have now':—or, to push it
to its extreme import,—'You sin now, we shall sin by and by; we
would sin now, if we could; not being successful, we expect our
revenge to-morrow.'" Emerson thinks he exaggerates, but he
does not; there are many lives in which the sins include all the
pleasures.

The feeling that evil is justified if only great good be added,
has given rise to another theory which Emerson did not really
adopt, although he often pointed out the facts on which it rests.
This is the theory of progress; the promise, not of a heaven of
pleasure, but of a millennium on earth, or at least of a perpetual

melioration. This hope is now the consolation usually proposed for the evils of experience, and we must regret that Emerson was not more explicit in his treatment of it. He had a great abhorrence for controversy and insisted on leaving out the negative propositions; this habit certainly makes his style genial and sweet-tempered, but it has its "compensation" in a vague and irresponsible way of writing. He tells us himself that he was always insincere, for he knew that there were other moods. Thus, he says that fate involves melioration; but he saw that it involved deterioration as well. "No statement of the universe can have any soundness which does not admit its ascending effort"; yet Emerson's own statement emphasizes compensation, which is his expression for the fact that ground is lost as fast as it is gained. Of course there is a creative effort in nature which in some measure is ascending; there is an ascending effort in a tree, but only until it is full grown. There is an ascending effort in the animal world, and the worst races, as Emerson tells us, are dead; but the last race, man, must die too. Emerson was not one of those who saw in progress a new revelation. He asserted calmly that all times were alike. He saw in progress nothing but succession. The order of the procession may interest the spectator; but it changes nothing in the pageant. What difference does it make whether the worst races come first or last? From the point of view of the intellect, and as truth, both first and last exist forever. It is always true that they have existed or will exist; and the universe is richer for their being. This is the sense in which nothing is lost; the sense in which "the direction of the whole and of the parts is towards benefit." "This life of ours is stuck round with Egypt, Greece, Gaul, England, War, Colonization, Church, Court and Commerce, as with so many flowers and wild ornaments grave and gay. I will not make more account of them. I believe in Eternity." Nothing, perhaps, gives Emerson a better right to be called a philosopher than his freedom from the superstition of progress. Many superstitions were already discredited, but this one was, in a great measure, the religion of his time.

II

There seem to be two different ways of forming an idea of the sum of things, through sympathy and through contemplation. If we try to put ourselves in the place of every creature that has ever lived, and thus form a notion of the sum of all experience, we approach the universe through sympathy. If, on the other hand, we are more inclined to reflection, our idea of the universe will be formed by looking at our own experience, as well as on that of others, from the outside; in this way we are compelled to regard inanimate nature, because we cannot imagine what experiences plants and rocks can have. If we extend our method of regarding these things to the animal world and to society, we form an idea of the universe as a great picture; this is what Emerson means by looking at things from the point of view of the intellect, or as truth; and this is the aspect of things he likes to dwell upon. To some minds it may seem unnatural to say that we see things as truth when we see them as imagination; some would say that the truth of a life was the series of experiences, not the series of attitudes; but Emerson means by truth not the real as experienced, but the ideal as conceived or remembered. He passes easily from all points of view to that of the intellect; and to this fact, more than to anything else, we owe his optimism.

Emerson's position is not that of simple idealism. The world as idea, for most philosophers, includes all experience; our pain and joy, anger and love, seem to them presentations to the mind as much as the landscape. But Emerson's idealism is double; there is in the first place the experience, and then, with time and reflection, comes the perception of the nature of that experience. Not the sight or emotion, but the description of them, is the truth. The primary use of a fact, he tells us, is low; the secondary use, as it is a figure or illustration of my thought, is the real worth. "The new deed is yet a part of life,—remains for a time immersed in our unconscious life. In some contemplative hour, it detaches itself from the life like a ripe fruit, to become a thought of the mind. Instantly it is raised, transfigured; the corruptible has put on incorruption. Henceforth it is an object of beauty, however base its origin and neighborhood. Observe, too, the impossibility of antedating this act. In the grub state, it cannot fly, it cannot shine; it is a dull grub. But suddenly, without observation, the self-same thing unfurls beautiful wings, and is an angel of wisdom. So is there no fact, no event in our private history, which shall not, sooner or later, lose its adhesive, inert form, and astonish us by soaring from our body into the empyrean. Cradle and infancy, school and playground, the fear of boys, and dogs, and ferules, the love of little maids and berries, and many another fact that once filled the whole sky, are gone already; friend and relative, profession and party, town and country, nation and world, must also soar and sing."

If felicity of expression is sufficient for us, surely we need add nothing to these words. But at the risk of degrading the thought, we must endeavor to define it; we must insist on knowing the conditions under which the great apparition shines so peacefully. Not every event or person pleases by being remote. Wars and persecutions, famine and leprosy, are less easily transfigured than the fear of dogs and ferules; they may be remote, but they do not on that account fill us with rapture. It is hard to put away the thought that they have been experiences; it is hard to look at them from the point of view of the intellect. Nevertheless, battle pieces make fine pictures and tragedies fine plays. If we wish, for example, to look at the Piedmontese Massacre as a truth, we must forget its low primary use, and even its secondary use in horrifying Milton, and think only of its use as a figure and illustration of Milton's thought, as a sonnet. Then, indeed, the massacre will soar and sing.

Aesthetic satisfaction counts for much in Emerson's optimism. It can be derived from any spectacle, if we but put sympathy aside. Sympathy, after all, is in most cases artificial. The unsophisticated man is quick to see the picturesqueness of the lights and shadows of life, so long as the shadow does not fall on him. We should all think a man morbid who refused to admire a plant, because he believe[d] it had grown so fine by destroying others. We should think a man at least over-sensitive who should refuse to praise the invention of torpedoes. Why, then, should [we] not admire the whole creation, that great invention of weapons and of armor?

But there is an element in Emerson's optimism even more important than delight in beauty, namely, religious faith. This series of events, this great picture, is nothing but a symbol and expression of "the Soul." The Soul not only looks through each of us, as through so many eyes, at the great panorama, but it paints the panorama at the same time. The world is not an aggregate but a unity; enveloping all imperfections in a perfect whole. "All loss, all pain, is particular; the universe remains to the heart unhurt. . . . For it is only the finite that has wrought and

suffered; the infinite lies stretched in smiling repose." To say, as
Emerson continually says, that the Soul is one and creates the
world, is to say that the world is rational and that if we could
understand it, we should see that it is very good.

But were this faith merely a puzzled trust, invoked because
other explanations of the world did not present themselves, it
would carry us but a little way towards optimism. A rigid Calvinist can hardly be called an optimist, yet he also believes that
everything happens according to the will of a God whose justice
and wisdom are not to be questioned. Thus he cuts the Gordian
knot by invoking mystery, and maintaining that it was good in
God to make an evil world. The terrifying expressions which the
Calvinist uses do not create a new difficulty; they only bring out
a difficulty which exists in every system that teaches that the
world is governed by reason. If a wise God can inflict any pain,
not our sense of justice, but only our pusillanimity, can lead us to
quarrel about the amount.

If Emerson had stopped with the assertion that there is a God,
he would have told us that we ought to be optimists, without
doing much to make us so. But he was not satisfied with a blind
faith; he tried to gain some insight into the mystery. Mysticism
may not be the soundest part of his philosophy, but it is at least
the soundest part of his optimism.

Just as experience has its mode of looking at the world, and by
sympathy tends to realize the sum of all lives; just as reflection
has its point of view and thinks of the universe as a great
spectacle; so the mystic has his peculiar vision, and by identi-
fying himself ideally with the power that created all things,
regards the world as the effect of his own will. In his moments of
union with the infinite, he has no need of promises of future
pleasures to make him forget his present ills; for he does not wish
to forget them. He need not wait until events and persons retire
to such a distance as to please the eye; for he does not care if
they please or not. To his eye the ugly is beautiful, since it is
God's work. To him pain is as welcome as pleasure, since both
come from the same source. Like the Stoics he thinks nothing evil
which is according to nature; like St. Francis he gives thanks for
"our sister, the death of the body"; to every natural force, to
every scourge and tribulation, he cries out like Shelley, "Be thou
me, impetuous one!" "The simplest person who in his integrity

worships God, becomes God. . . . How dear, how soothing to man, arises the idea of God, peopling the lonely place, effacing the scars of our mistakes and disappointments! . . . It inspires in man an ineffable trust. He has not the conviction, but the sight, that the best is the true . . . O, believe as thou livest, that every sound that is spoken over the round world, which thou oughtest to hear, will vibrate on thine ear! . . . Every friend whom not thy fantastic will, but the great and tender heart in thee craveth, shall lock thee in his embrace. And this because the heart in thee is the heart in all; not a valve, not a wall, not an intersection is there anywhere in nature, but one blood rolls uninterruptedly an endless circulation through all men, as the water of the globe is all one sea, and, truly seen, its tide is one."

All this may seem unintelligible; yet behind the rhetoric is a very definite meaning. "My fantastic will" stands for what I happen to desire; "the great and tender heart in me" stands for what I happen to get. The teaching is that what I happen to get comes to me according to an older and mightier law than my own will; and that it is better that my history should unfold itself according to that law than according to my selfish whim. We should not expect the world to be such as we would have made it; and the evil that comes in the name of the Lord is more blessed than any good coming in our own name. After all, the mystic makes the zeal the test of the ideal, in order to leave nothing unideal in the world; he declares that might is right, in order to banish wrong.

When Emerson announces this doctrine, he knows he will be charged with saying that "our crimes may be lively stories out of which we shall construct the temple of the true God." He admits that the charge ought to be brought against him; it is only his wife that keeps him from antinomianism. "But," says he, "let me remind the reader that I am only an experimenter. Do not set the least value on what I do—as if I pretended to settle anything as true or false. I unsettle all things. No facts are to me sacred, none are profane; I simply experiment, an endless seeker, with no Past at my back." This is pretty playfulness; a charming kind of self-satisfied humility; but Emerson does himself injustice. His doctrine of the oneness of things is no whim, but the soul of his philosophy. He repeats it over and over again, and does not fail to say some good words even for that enemy of the household, called antinomianism. Indeed, unless we admit that suffering and wrong are a necessary and desirable part of the scheme of things, our optimism does not deserve the name; and we need not be afraid of the consequences of saying that it must needs be that offence come, if we do not forget to add, "But woe unto him by whom the offence cometh."

The philosophical ground, then, of Emerson's optimism is his doctrine that one power produces all things, and therefore that all things have an equal right to be. There is a difference in creatures in the fulness and clearness with which they embody the Soul; this, Emerson says, is the radical tragedy in nature, the tragedy of more and less; but to the noble mind there is nothing sad in such a tragedy. Why should a fish have wings, or a brute reason? This is the objection of envy; a generous man will rejoice in the excellence of another. Why should the poor and suffering envy the prosperous? To be the most wretched of men is as high an honor before God as to be the happiest. For in ourselves we are nothing; we are so much vital force drawn from the infinite.

> "If the red slayer think he slays,
>   Or if the slain think he is slain,
> They know not well the subtle ways
>   I keep, and pass, and turn again.
>
> .   .   .   .
>
> They reckon ill who leave me out;
>   When me they fly, I am the wings;
> I am the doubter and the doubt,
>   And I the hymn the Brahmin sings."

III

If the account we have given of Emerson's optimism is at all correct, we might be tempted to doubt whether Emerson is an optimist at all. He finds the experience of the individual melancholy; he disdains the hope of a life of pleasure beyond the grave; and he makes little account of progress. His metaphysics teach us that there is one Soul, forever seeking to express itself in the phenomena of the universe, and at the same time contemplating its work as well as the idea on which the work is modelled. This doctrine Emerson announces in the most cheerful and poetic language; but the doctrine itself has nothing optimistic about it; nay, it is practically identical with the metaphysics of

Schopenhauer, the great apostle of pessimism. In one respect, indeed, the attitudes of these two are opposed; for Emerson, in his mysticism, identifies himself with the creative power and submits his reason to the intoxication of that union; but Schopenhauer, while he recognizes the identity of his own will and the universal, yet keeps his judgment aloof and allows it to condemn the work of the will. Emerson's view seems the more rational, although it necessitates the surrender of reason; because the faculty of judging whether things are good or evil, being itself a product of the creative power, is not competent to pass judgment on that power. A mystical union with God, in which the judgment remains in abeyance, is the ultimate attitude of the soul; and the insight thus gained has higher authority than the critical faculty.

Between Emerson, then, and a pessimist like Schopenhauer there is a fundamental opposition; yet this opposition alone hardly entitles Emerson to the name of optimist. The Stoics, the mystics, and Spinoza take Emerson's view, yet we do not think of them as optimists. Shall we say that Emerson was more consistent or more profound than these? Why this striking difference in the tone of men with the same inspiration? Surely neither Plato, nor the Christian Saints, nor Marcus Aurelius, nor anyone with whom Emerson's philosophy seems to associate him, walked this earth with a bland and persistent smile. Can it be that they all nursed childish and petulant griefs? or did they learn something from that sorrow which Emerson says can teach us nothing?

It is not Emerson's philosophy that makes him an optimist, but his character. His thought, to use his own expression, is a train of moods like a string of beads, and temperament the iron wire on which the beads are strung. The first thing that we feel in Emerson is his distance from the working day world; he speaks from afar off. His writing is concrete and poetic; but for one who takes such delight in mentioning miscellaneous objects, he leaves on the reader's mind a sense of strange unreality. He listens to the hum of human life as to the humble-bee, and looks on wars as on the bursting of thunderclouds. Had he shared the doctrine of the extreme idealists who believe that they alone exist, he could not have been more self-contained. He was not unamiable; he treated all men well, treated them as if they were real; "perhaps," said he, "they are." But even the possibility of their existence could not disturb him; his own troubles did not disturb him much, why should other people's? If men felt sick and sorry, they had but to look at the stars; let them consider the splendid bounty of nature, and see the impertinence of their griefs. As for him, to lose a dear child was to lose a beautiful estate, and nothing more: a picture had been taken from his wall. The only thing sorrow could teach him was how unreal it was; and he grieved that grief could teach him nothing. Grief being so distressingly unreal, there was no excuse for "grumbling, discontented people. I know those miserable fellows" he says, "and I hate them. . . . When the political economist reckons up the unproductive classes, he should put at the head this class of pitiers of themselves, cravers of sympathy, bewailing imaginary disasters." "There is one topic peremptorily forbidden to all well bred, to all rational mortals, namely, their distempers. If you have not slept, or if you have slept, or if you have headache, or sciatica, or leprosy, or thunderstroke, I beseech you, by all angels, to hold your peace, and not pollute the morning to which all the housemates bring serene and pleasant thoughts, by corruption and groans."

To this moderate sympathy with the aches and sores of the unphilosophical, Emerson joins no small contempt for their lives. "In the streets we grow cynical. The men we meet are coarse and torpid. The finest wits have their sediment. What quantities of fribbles, paupers, invalids, epicures, antiquaries, politicians, thieves, and triflers of both sexes might be advantageously spared! . . . A person seldom falls sick but the bystanders are animated with a faint hope that he will die:—quantities of poor lives; of distressing invalids; of cases for a gun. . . . The worst of charity is that the lives you are asked to preserve are not worth preserving. Masses! the calamity is the masses. I do not wish any mass at all, but honest men only, lovely, sweet, accomplished women only, and no shovel-handed, narrow-brained, gin-drinking million stockingers or lazzaroni at all." And the better class itself is not of much account. "I cannot recall any form of man who is not superfluous sometimes. But is not this pitiful? Life is not worth the taking, to do tricks in." And yet, "I find my account in sots and bores also. They give a reality to the circumjacent picture which such a vanishing, meteorous appearance can ill spare." So that if we are "poised, and wise, and our own today," and watch good humoredly the tricks that others do, life may be worth taking after all.

Here we see—and this is Emerson's least respectable side—the mystic turned dilettante. When this half-seriousness, this supercilious satisfaction betray themselves, Emerson loses our confidence. Yet his avowed playfulness has its charm; his gentle contempt of men and things has its root in a philosophic habit of mind. The companion of nature, the lover of eternal things, must think social cares and ambitions trivial. To feel their insignificance is to be spiritually-minded. It is true that those who have been great as well as spiritual, have known how to reconcile their lofty wisdom with the spirit of sacrifice and with infinite pity for their fellow-men. But we like Emerson none the worse for not being a hero nor a saint; he has his own inimitable charm; his very indifference is delightful. "Nature will not have us fret and fume. She does not like our benevolence or our learning much better than she likes our frauds and wars. When we come out of the caucus, or the bank, or the abolition-convention, or the temperance-meeting, or the transcendental club, into the fields and woods, she says to us, 'So hot? my little Sir.'"

To do justice to the personal element in Emerson's optimism we should have to study his whole life. We should have to inquire whether he ever felt an emotion stronger than delight in the landscape, and decide whether his serenity was the result of discipline or of insensibility. But we must leave such matters to his biographers, and content ourselves with what we can gather from his writings. These, however, can leave us little doubt that the man is the most important element in the doctrine; and that, in accordance with his own precept, he is never a philosopher, but always Emerson philosophizing. If he made no account of experience it was not so much that he saw a reason for disregarding it, as that he did not find it an engaging subject. If the world as idea is his constant theme, it is so because it pleases him, not because he is convinced that there is no other philosophical way of regarding the world. Emerson would not have denied this; he would have been proud to plead guilty to the charge of viewiness; there is no attitude he was so anxious to avoid as that of the doctrinaire. And accordingly his optimism is not so much a doctrine as a tendency: a quick eye for beauty, a turning aside from pain and sorrow, a mystical elevation of spirit. We find in

Emerson many encouraging words, much perception of the beauty and excellence of things; and we must be dull and morbid indeed, if we are not charmed by so much sweetness and serenity. But to those who are not yet free from the troublesome feelings of pity and shame, Emerson brings no comfort; he is the prophet of a fair-weather religion.

EMERSON'S POEMS PROCLAIM THE DIVINITY OF NATURE, WITH FREEDOM AS HIS PROFOUNDEST IDEAL

The New England on which Emerson opened his eyes was a singular country. It manifested in an acute form something not yet quite extinct in America—the phenomenon of an old soul in a new body.

The inevitable simplicity of the new life was a part of its virtue, and its accidental isolation seemed a symbol of divine election and the harbinger of a new era of righteousness.

But no such pleasing reflections could remove the anomaly of an old soul in a young body, an anomaly much too violent to last. The dogmas which Calvinism had chosen for interpretation were the most sombre and disquieting in the Christian system, those which marked most clearly a broken life and a faith rising out of profound despair. But what profound despair or what broken life could exist in young America to give meaning and truth to those spectral traditions? People who looked and thought for themselves, people who yearned for that deeper sincerity which comes from shaking off verbal habits and making belief a direct expression of instinct and perception, challenged at last their ancestral

---

This is the text of an address delivered at Harvard during Emerson Memorial Week, Friday, May 22, 1903. It was published in the "Special Emerson Supplement," *Boston Daily Advertiser*, May 23, 1903.

dream, threw off its incubus, rubbed their eyes, as it were, in the
morning light, and sprang into the world of nature.

In no man was this awakening more complete than in Emerson. No one greeted it with greater joy or recognized more
quickly his inward affinity to nature rather than to the artificial
moral world in which he had been reared. The scales dropped of
themselves from his eyes and left his vision as pure and clear as if
no sophistications had ever existed in the world. The instinct
which took him at one leap into the bosom of reality, and
brought him face to face with unbiased experience, is the greatest evidence of his genius, or perhaps we should say, of his
simplicity; for he shed the incrustations of time, not by a long
and mighty effort of reflection, not by a laborious sympathetic
progress through all human illusions, but rather by a native
immunity and a repulsion on his part. Other people's troubles
could not adhere to him; he remained like a grain of sand, clean
and whole in any environment. This simplicity clarified and
disinfected the world for him as only the ripest wisdom could
disinfect or clarify it for other men. How singular his privilege
was in this respect, our own time may easily convince us, when
we still find almost everybody entangled in all sorts of reticences
and fears, trying to cover up nature's face, to disallow her laws,
to supplement her gifts with contraband goods, or to turn her
bodily upside down by some metaphysical artifice. Emerson had
a plentiful mysticism of his own, but it was spontaneous, fanciful,
ingenuous; when a spirit has wings it needs no acrobatic system
of philosophy. Natural activities and natural sentiments may
have found some checks in Emerson's character and training, but
nature herself wore no veils to his mind. His emancipation from
tradition, in so far as the march of things is concerned, was
entire. He retained no weakness for a sacred geography which is
not exactly geography, or a sacred history which is not quite
history. His world was the world of scientific observation and
practical life; Spinoza's universe could hardly be more natural,
nor Shakespeare's more unfalsified, nor Goethe's more liberal and
large. What such men achieved by intellectual power, or just
imagination or acquaintance with life, Emerson attained by his
innate and happy simplicity. He had but to open his eyes, and
although what happened to offer itself to his glance may have

lacked richness and volume and although his observation itself
may have been desultory, yet he was a born master at looking
deep and at looking straight.

But it is time we should ask ourselves what these direct and
searching glances were fixed upon. Sometimes they rested on
human life, but more often and far more lovingly on nature; for
even when human life was the theme it was generally conceived
as one more effluence and illustration of universal laws, and
seldom from the point of view of positive human interests. The
love of nature was Emerson's strongest passion; no other influence swayed him so often, stirred him so deeply, or made him
so truly a poet. If he regarded any moral or political problem
with sympathetic or steady attention, he immediately stated it in
terms of some natural analogy and escaped its importunity and
finality by imagining what nature, in such a conflict, would pass
to next. What seems mysticism in his moral philosophy and
baffles the reader who is looking for a moral solution, is nothing
but this rooted habit of inattention to what is not natural law,
natural progression, natural metamorphosis. Interest and delight
in that spectacle overmasters every other feeling, so lovingly and
sympathetically has its detail been observed, so grandly have its
wider harmonies been imagined.

All Emerson's compositions are woven of mixed threads, and
resemble the universe of Anaxagoras, where everything was
bound to contain every kind of substance. But perhaps the purest
gold to be gleaned from all these quarries is what, borrowing a
title from one of the poems, we may call collectively "woodnotes," verses inspired by blithe, attentive, rapturous perception
of all the shifts and postures of natural things—plants, birds,
skies, waters—by sympathetic immersion in those processes, by
refreshment drawn from such vicarious elemental living. These
woodnotes are full of tenderness, humor, a pleasing mythical
fancy, perhaps a tendency to trace rather fantastic analogies and
to proclaim identity in things tolerably remote from one another;
but we are free for the time being from mystical negations and
artificial enigmas. The dominant note of exultation is not the
forced optimism of a doctrinaire; it is a natural joy in joy, in
variety, in harmony, in the affinities and wide suggestions of
things; the observation is observation of fact, of movement, of

things describable and characteristic. Sometimes this sympathy
with nature actually breaks through the film of New England
prudery and we read that

> "Good fellow Puck and goblins
>   Know more than any book. . . .
> The south winds are quick-witted
>   The schools are sad and slow,
> The masters quite omitted
>   The lore we care to know."

It is useless to describe what is itself description, and quotation
would carry us too far if we were to repeat all the woodnotes or
echo every phase of nature which they celebrate. One remark,
however, before leaving this most delightful part of our subject:
Emerson's love of nature was honest and unreserved; it was
founded on nature's irresistible charm, grace, power, infinity. It
was sincere adoration, self-surrendering devotion; it was not
qualified or taken back by any subsumption of nature under
human categories, as if after all she were nothing but her children's instrument, illusion or toy. "Dearest nature," as he calls her,
remained for him always a mother, a fountain not only of inspiration but of life. The spiritual principle he discovered in her was
her own spirit, which man, being a bubble in her stream, might
well breathe in for a moment and joyfully share; but it was she
that the more deeply inspired. She was the mistress and sibyl, he
the pupil, the trembling interpreter of her oracles. Firmly, even
arrogantly, as Emerson could assert his spiritual freedom in the
face of men and human tradition, in nature's presence he had no
transcendental conceit. For this reason his poetry about nature,
though fanciful as such poetry may well be, remains always
receptive, always studied from life and free from sentimental
impertinence.

When he idealizes most, he is still striving only to comprehend.
If we compare, for instance, his way of feeling the landscape
with Wordsworth's way, we shall see that he is less inclined to
fall into the pathetic fallacy. Emerson's transcendentalism, had
he borrowed it from scholastic systems, might have given him a
technical right to treat nature as a figment put together by man's
ingenuity for man's convenience; but he respected her too much
to impute to her so much respect for man; he saw her as she
really is and loved her in her indomitable and inhuman perfec-

tion. Not the least of his joys was the self-effacing one of being able to conceive, and therefore to share, a life which creates, animates and destroys the human. He was charmed and comforted, quite without technical apparatus, by universal beauty. He yielded himself insensibly and placidly to that plastic stress which in breeding new forms out of his substance would never breed anything alien to those principles of harmony and rhythm which stand like sentinels at the gates of being and challenge the passage into existence of anything contradicting itself or incongruous with its natural conditions. His best lyric flights express this honest and noble acceptance of destiny, this imaginative delight in innumerable beauties which he should never see, but which would be the heirs of those he had loved and lost in their passage. So in the lines entitled Pan:

> "O, what are heroes, prophets, men,
> But pipes through which the breath of Pan doth blow
> A momentary music. Being's tide
> Swells hitherward, and myriads of forms
> Live, robed with beauty, painted by the sun;
> Their dust, pervaded by the nerves of God,
> Throbs with an overmastering energy,
> Knowing and doing. Ebbs the tide, they lie
> White hollow shells upon the desert shore.
> But not the less the eternal wave rolls on
> To animate new millions, and exhale
> Races and planets, its enchanted foam."

In another place he represents the poet, troubled by premonitions of his own weakness and mortality, who says:

> "Is there warrant that the waves
> Of Thought in their mysterious caves
> Will heap in me their highest tide,
> In me therewith beatified?
> Unsure the ebb and flood of thought.
> The moon comes back; the spirit not."

And the spirits reply:—

> "Brother, no decrepitude
> Chills the limbs of Time;
>
> . . . .
> On nature's wheels there is no rust,
> Nor less on man's enchanted dust
> Beauty and Force alight."

And again, in "Woodnotes" proper:—

"When the forest shall mislead me,
When the night and morning lie,
When the sea and land refuse to feed me,
'Twill be time enough to die.
Then will yet my mother yield
A pillow in her greenest field
Nor the June flowers scorn to cover
The clay of their departed lover."

But however beautiful and miraculous the summer woods might seem, or however fascinating those circles, laws, surfaces, and compensations of which the cosmos was full, there must be other elements in a poet's inspiration. All men of letters in the 19th century have been inclined to love and describe nature; but this somewhat novel theme has entered an imagination filled already with other matters, preoccupied, perhaps, with political or religious revolutions. A moral and human substratum, a national and personal idiosyncrasy, has existed in every case and has furnished a background for the new vision of nature; and it makes a great difference in a poet whether behind the naturalist in him there lies, for instance, a theologian, a statesman, or an artist. In Emerson what lay behind the naturalist was in a measure a political thinker, a moralist interested in institutions and manners, a democrat and a Puritan; but chiefly what lay there was a mystic, a moralist athirst for some superhuman and absolute good. The effect of this situation upon his poetry is what remains for us to consider.

Nothing in all Emerson's writings is more eloquent and popular than some bits of his patriotic verse. There are not only the Concord and Boston hymns, but sparks of the same fire shoot out in other places; for Emerson could not have written so well upon occasion, I may almost say to order, if he had not been full already of the enthusiasm which that occasion demanded. Art or a merely sympathetic imagination never dictated a line to this Puritan bard, who if he was perfectly bland was also absolutely unyielding and self-directed. No force affected him save those which made him up. Freedom, in its various expressions, was his profoundest ideal, and if there was anything which he valued more than the power to push on to what might lie before, it was the power to escape what lay behind. A sense of potentiality and a sense of riddance are, as he might have said, the two poles of liberty. In America both poles were highly magnetic, for here, more than elsewhere, old things had been thrown off and new things were to be expected. Potentiality, cosmic liberty, nature perpetually transforming and recovering her energy, formed his loftiest theme; but the sense of riddance in escaping kings, churches, cities, and eventually self and even humanity, was the nearer and if possible the livelier emotion.

The verses which he devoted to memories of the Revolutionary War and to the agitation against slavery, though brief, are the most thrilling and profound which those themes have yet inspired. Everybody knows of the "embattled farmers" who "fired the shot heard round the world." Perhaps less present to the younger generation are his stirring lines, in which he denounced slavery and dreamt of the negro's future.

> "Pay ransom to the owner
> And fill the bag to the brim.
> Who is the owner? The slave is owner
> And ever was. Pay him."

And while the master was thus bitterly challenged, the slave was idealized:—

> "He has avenues to God
> Hid from men of northern brain,
> Far beholding, without cloud,
> What these with slowest steps attain.

> If once the generous chief arrive
> To lead him, willing to be led,
> For freedom he will strike and strive
> And drain his heart till he be dead."

We need not ask whether verses like these have a place in literature: it is certain that they have a place in American history and put vividly before us the passions of a momentous hour.

But Emerson's love of freedom did not need crying abuses to kindle it to flame; it was a speculative love that attached him to whatever was simple, untrammelled, idyllic in any time or sphere.

As he detested what he called the "fopperies of the town," so he detested the fopperies of history; Europe made him only a better American. In the verses entitled "The Park" we see how his "conscience masterful," his "sentiment divine against the being of

a line," found those he calls "the prosperous and beautiful"
somehow unnatural and distinctly ungodly, as if they were too
much exempt from the universal purifying flux; and he prized his
titmouse's

> "Wiry chant
> O'er all that mass or minster vaunt."

Jehovah, too, he was sure, had of late become a leveller, for he
said:—

> "I am tired of kings.
> I suffer them no more. . . .
> I will have never a noble,
> No lineage counted great,
> Fishers and choppers and ploughmen
> Shall constitute a state.
> Go cut down the trees in the forest
> And build me a wooden house."

Wooden houses, or better still log cabins, were indeed Emerson's sacred architecture; and when he wished to excuse himself
for not loving very much even the Boston of his day, he expressed
his aversion by referring to it generally as "the marble town." A
town, even if largely in wood, had not only the disadvantage of
not being the country, but also that of being something arrested
and immovable. Its potentiality seemed to be exhausted, and the
mind dwelling there was not free. Freedom was thus associated
with space rather than with action. To one whose life flowed so
predominantly from within to have room was already to have
enough opportunity, and he was more afraid of hindrance than of
starvation.

The same general temper appears in all he says about love and
friendship. A too great refinement and dread of intrusion seems
to attenuate these feelings, yet it is only excessive sensitiveness
that produces this appearance of frigidity. "Hast thou," he says in
"Forbearance":

> "Hast thou loved so well a high behavior
> In man or maid that thou from speech refrainedst
> Nobility more nobly to repay?
> O be my friend and teach me to be thine!"

And again:—

> "I have no brothers and no peers
> And the dearest interferes.

> When I would spend a lonely day
> Sun and moon are in the way."

We are here at the frontiers of that province in Emerson's kingdom into which it is hardest to penetrate—the forbidden Thibet, with its Grand Lama, behind his Himalayas. When our philosopher substituted nature for the theological cosmos, and nature's magic providence for God's, he did not in the least feel that he had surrendered anything of spiritual value, anything that altered his personal religion or even his Christianity. This may seem an irrational persistence of habitual sentiments after the objects that aroused them have disappeared. But religion is not so simple a matter. It is not at bottom an account of credible facts producing, when duly reported, saving emotions in the soul. It is rather an expression of the soul's native emotions in symbols mistaken for facts, or in facts chosen for symbols. At least this is what religion was for Emerson, as for everybody who envisages things in the transcendental manner and reduces everything to its fighting weight in his own mental arena. Hence, if one set of symbols is substituted for another, nothing is changed in the thing signified, in the inner life of the soul, except the vehicle of expression. All the unction and sanctity of religion may then survive its dogmas; for the meaning they once had for life is now transferred to other ideas. All ideas, we presently perceive, are fluid; and we are on the point of venturing the assertion that it matters very little what things exist or how long they endure, since the only reality is the perpetual motion that creates, transforms, and exchanges them. We have seen how this perpetual motion, observable in nature, fascinated Emerson; but while the poet could justify and communicate his delight by dwelling on the forms and beauties of things in transition, the metaphysician would fain sink deeper. In his desperate attempt to seize upon the real and permanent he would fain grasp and hold fast the disembodied principle of change itself. This idea, loaded with religious passion, is one Emerson often attempted to put in verse.

> "I tire of shams, I rush to be.
> I pass with yonder comet free,
> Pass with the comet into space."

"The lords of life, the lords of life, I saw them pass," says new-born man, awed by his gigantic visions; and nature, "dearest nature, strong and kind," consoles him:—

> "Darling, never mind.
> Tomorrow they will wear another face.
> The founder thou. These are thy race."

Again, at the end of "Threnody":—

> "Revere thy Maker; fetch thine eye
> Up to his style and manners of the sky.
> Not of adamant and gold
> Built he heaven stark and cold.
> No, but a nest of bending reeds,
> Flowering grass and scented weeds.
>
> . . . .
>
> Built of tears and sacred flames
> And virtue reaching to its aims;
> Built of furtherance and pursuing,
> Not of spent deeds but of doing.
> Silent rushes the swift Lord
> Through ruined systems still restored.
>
> . . . .
>
> House and tenant go to ground,
> Lost in God, in Godhead found."

And in the well-known Brahma:—

> "If the red slayer think he slays
> Or if the slain think he is slain,
> They know not well the subtle ways
> I keep and pass and turn again.
>
> Far and forgot to me is near;
> Shadow and sunlight are the same;
> The vanished gods to me appear;
> And one to me are shame and fame."

The images, insofar as images exist here, are not different from those of "Woodnotes"; all is still a description of the natural world and its revolutions. Only now our emotion is differently directed. There we dwelt on particular things; we heard that

> "A woodland walk,
> A guest of river-grapes, a mocking thrush,
> A wild rose or rock-loving columbine,
> Salve all my wounds."

Now, instead of these definite images, we are asked to

> "Melt matter into dreams,
> Panoramas which I saw,

And whatever glows or seems,
Into substance, into Law."

If now we try to bring to a focus this desultory survey, what shall we see in Emerson's poetic achievement? Briefly this: his verses put together in a more pungent and concentrated form his guiding ideas. They are filled with high thought, enthusiasm, terseness; they contain snatches of lyric beauty. Their total burden is not distinguishable from that of the author's essays. This burden is repeated with many variations and transpositions; and the secret of understanding it consists in seeing that its changing expressions are complementary and not mutually exclusive. What exists in nature infinitely deployed exists potentially at every moment in each of her parts; so that these parts, finding the whole latent in themselves and their own soul latent in every other thing, are able to understand one another and the whole world, in proportion as they advance in self-knowledge.

The poems render this philosophy, as is natural, in its most picturable form. They proclaim the divinity of nature, and her immortal fecundity in all her kinship with man, things which the human spirit might recognize to be beautiful and good if keyed to heroism and rapt in contemplation. Undoubtedly the beauty they celebrate involves cruelty, and the optimism they preach demands abnegation. We may even add that such a continual hymn to nature's fluid harmonies allows us to forget altogether that laborious progress, that architecture of reason and art, which is after all nature's masterpiece and which alone enables us to appreciate her other works. For that man must have a long civilization behind him who has learned to love nature for her own sake.

But when allowance is made for such partialities as no philosopher and no prophet was ever free from, what more sacred and delightful fountain of truth can we find anywhere than that which bubbles in this spirit? In an age that is putting off its traditional faiths and assuming instead innumerable material burdens, who can be more welcome than a thinker to whom all the sanctions of faith are inseparable from reason and all the forms of matter instinct with beauty and mind? Such a guide points in the direction of hope, he leads in the way of ultimate benefit. For as we sprang from earth and yet found that we were spirits, so by a further conquest and dominion over matter, both in thought and in action, we may enlarge that grandeur to which our dust is allied. We need but to dominate our follies and make ourselves at home in our own house. And who will say that this is impossible?

> "When reason whispers low, Thou must,
> The heart replies: I can."

WALT WHITMAN: A DIALOGUE

McStout. Coming?

Van Tender. What, is it time?

McStout. Fifteen minutes before the game begins. We might take a stroll. It is such splendid weather!

Van Tender. Yes, and this is the best place to enjoy it. The warm wind blows in over you, and you can almost fancy how the trees feel when they thaw, and the sap begins to run, and the buds throb till they burst, and every leaf breathes and trembles. The plants don't have to move from their places to feel that it's spring. Why should we? You know my motto:

> "Better than to stand to sit, better than to sit to lie,
> Better than to dream to sleep, better than to sleep to die."

But you can't expect to attain the highest good at one bound from the depths of Philistia. You can't do better for the present than to come in and stretch your energetic self on the other half of the window seat. Isn't it delicious? What better apology for idlers? Here you can breathe the air and look at the fresh grass, while you read a poet and cut a lecture. He tells you how in

---

This piece appeared in *The Harvard Monthly,* May, 1890.

another country, perhaps, he felt what you are feeling now, as he watched the spring of another year. That is the best part of the pleasure, to know that it's human, and that all men have had it in common, from Adam down.

McStout. And who is your poet now? Swinburne?

Van Tender. Oh, no.

McStout. Keats?

Van Tender. No; it's Walt Whitman. There is a time for everything, you know.

McStout. If, like you, one does nothing. No wonder you like Walt Whitman now and then for a change. You must be so tired of poetry.

Van Tender. Isn't this poetry? What is poetry?

McStout. A matter of words—more of words than matter. But if Walt Whitman is poetry, it isn't on account of the words. You don't pretend he can write English?

Van Tender. Not according to the English department. But that is a local standard. Could Homer pass an examination in Goodwin's moods and tenses? And doesn't he say Σμινθεῦ, which is a ἅπαξ λεγόμενου?[1]

McStout. I dare say Homer talked as it was the fashion to talk in his day. And when English becomes a dead language and nothing survives but the *Leaves of Grass*, Whitman's style will be above criticism. But now English has the misfortune of being in use. A man can't make it to suit his fancy, and if he won't trouble himself to write the language of his fellows he can't expect them to learn his. How can you endure a man who has neither the accent of Christians, nor the style of a Christian, pagan, nor man?

Van Tender. Precisely for that reason: he produces a new effect, he gives you a new sensation. If you will show me a well-written book that contains the same emotion, I agree to bind the leaves of grass into bundles and cast them into the furnace. If only a man could become an artist in his words, and yet retain the innocence of his feelings! But to learn a method of expression is to become insensible to all it can't express. The schools don't

---

[1] Smintheus (god of mice or destroyer of mice) is an epithet for Apollo, used by Homer in *The Iliad*, Book I, line 39. Van Tender's witticism turns on a doubt that Homer's use of the vocative case would be acceptable to Professor Goodwin.

teach us to paint what we see, but to see what others have painted.

McStout. I've heard of an old master who used to say to his pupils, "Copy if you want to be copied." When people are fascinated by the extravagant they show they haven't experience and training enough to appreciate what is sane and solid. Would you make no distinction between the normal and human and the eccentric and perverse? You toss sense and grammar to the Philistines, who ought to be correct since they can't be original. But your geniuses, you think, mustn't submit to standards; they create standards. If they didn't seem ridiculous to the vulgar, would they be truly sublime? You may say that if you like, but if originality is genius there are more great men at Somerville than at Cambridge. You can't get over the difference between sense and nonsense, between beauty and caprice. Any one can produce a new effect when fools are impressed by his blunders. You may like to hear Whitman's "barbaric yawp over the roofs of the world," but you must confess it is a whim of yours, and that a yawp is one thing and a poem another.

Van Tender. Certainly, I admit that a barbarism is an annoyance. When I come upon one it gives me a little shock, and I wish for the moment that it wasn't there. But there are models of English enough. I don't read Whitman for his verbal graces, although he has them, after his own fashion. If you wrote me a letter it might not be a model of style either, yet I should read it with interest if it told me what I wanted to hear. And Whitman does that. He hasn't the merits of Keats or of Shakspere, but he has merits of his own. His verses bring a message theirs couldn't bring, so I read theirs for their style and his for his inspiration. It is the voice of nature crying in the wilderness of convention.

McStout. I wish you could tell me what you mean by that. The only novelty I can see in him is that he mentions all sorts of things and says nothing about them. If you like pantheism and indecency, why aren't you satisfied with French novels and German philosophy? These are the same things in their genuine form.

Van Tender. It's not a theory or a description of things I get from Whitman. It's an attitude, a faculty of appreciation. You may laugh at his catalogues of objects, at his enumeration of places. But the hurrying of these images through the mind gives

me a sense of space, of a multiplicity of things spread endlessly
around me. I become aware of the life of millions of men, of
great stretches of marsh, desert, and ocean. Have you never
thought of the poetry of the planet? Fancy this little ball spinning
along so fast, and yet so little in a hurry. Imagine the film of
blue-gray water and the flat patches of land, now green, now
brown, and dim clouds creeping over all. And near the ocean,
here and there, conceive the troops of men and animals darken-
ing the earth like so many ants. And think how little the murmur
of one thousand jargons ruffles the air, and how the praises of
each god are drowned in the vaults of his temple!

McStout. But all that is very different from Walt Whitman.
Astronomy may have its impressive side, and even geography,
when you connect it with the fortunes of mankind. Science is
interesting, and if you can manage to make poetry out of it we
shall have the first poetry in the world not resting on illusion. It
seems to me that the illusion is what is poetic, and the fact is so
only when in fancy we assimilate it to the fiction. The migrations
of men from one land to another, for instance, are important
events, and you may cast the glamour of poetry over them for a
moment by dramatizing them. You may call the Strait of Magel-
lan a Hellespont and himself a Jason. You may say the whole
world is a Troad and the history of civilization a war of heroes.
But if you mention the heroes, and their real qualities, where is
the poetry? And if you reverse the process and try to explain the
fables as history symbolized, or what not, you degrade the ideal
and distort the facts. The reason why Walt Whitman is ridiculous
is that he talks of real objects as if they could enter into poetry at
all. It isn't art to point to objects, nor poetry to turn out "chants of
Ohio, Indiana, Illinois, Wisconsin, Iowa, and Minnesota." Poetry
deals with sensuous attractions, found nowhere on the map. To
see them you must have a passport into fairy land.

Van Tender. Ah, you are caught at last! You have defined
poetry. Now I wouldn't for a moment defend metaphysical con-
fusions. The trouble with the German sort of criticism is that it
isn't satisfied with the fact, but goes in search of a theory, as if a
theory could be anything real and ultimate, or more than the
flight of the soul from perception to perception, from emotion to
emotion, on which alone she can alight to find rest and truth.

"Grau, theurer Freund, ist alle Theorie,
Und grün des Lebens goldner Baum."[2]

But what makes you think the essence poetry distils can't be extracted from every object? Why should one thing leave its type in the world of ideas, and not another! Trust me, beauty is everywhere, if we only had the genius to see it. If a man has the ability to make us feel the fitness, the necessity, the beauty of common things, he is a poet of the highest type. If some objects seem to you poetic rather than others, if Venice can be apostrophised and Oshkosh is unmentionable, it's because habit makes it easier to idealize them. This beauty has been pointed out so often that we know it by heart. But what merit is it to repeat the old tricks, and hum the old tunes? You add nothing to the beauty of the world. You see no new vision. You are the author of nothing, but merely an apprentice in the poetic guild, a little poet sucking the honey with which great poets have sweetened words. You are inspired by tradition and judged by convention. Yet this very convention must have been inspiration at first. The real objects about a man must have impressed him and he must have found words fit to communicate his impression. These words in that way became poetic, and afterwards any man who used them was an artist.

McStout. And you think literary tradition wholly arbitrary? You think it a mere accident that all hearts were touched by one man's words, and that all generations adopted his words and imitated his methods? Why was one poet's inspiration turned into a convention rather than another's? Evidently because he discovered and selected the truly interesting aspects of life, and dwelt upon those things which of themselves are beautiful. Don't you know how every age fancies it has a poet of original genius, that afterwards turns out to have been nothing but a fashionable mountebank? He had some trick that appealed to a particular mood or passion of the time, and his success in drawing attention for the moment is mistaken for a sign of greatness. That happens to Walt Whitman. The times are favorable to his vague pantheism, his formlessness, his confusion of values, his substitu-

---

[2] "All theory, my friend, is grey,/But life's golden tree springs ever green." From Goethe, *Faust*, Part I, "Faust's Study," iii.

tion of emotion for thought, his trust in impulse rather than in experience. Because we are too ignorant or too wilful to see the distinctions of things and of persons, we decree that there are no distinctions, and proceed to remodel literature and society upon that principle.

Van Tender. If the distinctions are real, there is no danger of their being destroyed. Things have different values, as one star differs from another star in brightness. All I insist on is that in all you can see light, if your eyes are open. Whitman would teach you, if you would only read him, to see in things their intrinsic nature and life, rather than the utility they may have for one another. That is his great merit, his sublime justice. It is a kind of profound piety that recognizes the life of every thing in nature, and spares it, and worships its intrinsic worth. There is something brutal and fatuous in the habit we commonly have of passing the parts of nature in review and pronouncing them good or bad according to the effect they have on our lives. Aren't they as real as ourselves? In practical life we have to override them, for if we waited for justice and the ultimate good to direct what we should do, we should die before we had done anything. But it's the privilege of contemplation to be just. Listen to what Whitman says here:

"I do not call the tortoise unworthy because she is not something else,
And the jay in the woods never studied the gamut, yet trills pretty
    well to me,
And the look of the bay mare shames silliness out of me."

McStout. This justice of yours may be sublime, but isn't it a trifle dangerous? By admiring the beasts so much we may come to resemble them,—or perhaps the resemblance is the cause of the admiration. You may say it is brutal to make ourselves a standard for other creatures; yet a human standard is better than none at all, and can we have any other? But Walt Whitman, I understand, would think it a great improvement if men imitated the animals more than they do.

Van Tender. Undoubtedly, in some respects. Here he explains it perfectly:

"I think I could turn and live with animals, they are so placid and
    self-contained,
I stand and look at them long and long.
They do not sweat and whine about their condition,

They do not lie awake in the dark and weep for their sins,
They do not make me sick discussing their duty to God,
Not one is dissatisfied, not one is demented with the mania of owning
    things,
Not one kneels to another, nor to his kind that lived thousands of
    years ago,
Not one is respectable or unhappy over the whole earth."

McStout. And not one writes bad prose or worse poetry, not one is untrue to his instincts as all this talk is untrue to the better instincts of man.

Van Tender. I knew it would come at last: Walt Whitman is immoral!

McStout. It isn't immoral to call a spade a spade, but it is immoral to treat life as a masquerade, as a magic pantomime in which acts have no consequences and happiness and misery don't exist.

Van Tender. Ah, but Whitman is nothing if not a spectator, a cosmic poet to whom the whole world is a play. And good and evil, although not equally pleasant to experience, are equally interesting to look at. Is it wrong to enjoy our misery when its distance from us makes contemplation of it possible? How else can the gods have been happy? To refuse us this pleasure is to deprive us of a consolation without preventing our suffering. Or do you think the knowledge of what life is would make us unfit to live? Should we be really more wicked if the sun were not a Puritan and dared to look on the world through the twenty-four hours?

McStout. Perhaps not, but the trouble with your contemplation and impartiality is that it unnerves a man and makes him incapable of indignation or enthusiasm. He goes into raptures over everything, and accomplishes nothing. The world is so heavenly to him that he finds nothing to do in it.

Van Tender. Except play his harp and wear his crown. Is it nothing to perceive the beauty of the world, and help other men to perceive it? I don't mean simply the pleasure of art itself. I mean the widening of your sympathies, your reconciliation with nature. What better thing is there for a man than to remember now and then that the stars are laughing at him, to renounce his allegiance to his own preferences and passions and by understanding to enter into those of other men? We can't play at life without getting some knocks and bruises, and without running some chance of defeat. But our best moments are the breathing spells when we survey the field and see what a glorious game it all is.

McStout. I'm glad we may do that, especially as the other game is over.

Van Tender. What! is it possible we have been talking so long?

McStout. There are the men coming back. We've won, though. You can tell by their faces.

Van Tender. So you see we weren't really needed. For all our philosophy, the world wags on.

Part III

TRADITION AND PRACTICE

Editor's note: The little-known essay "Tradition and Practice" approaches the problem of the division between the American Intellect and Will in quite a different way from Santayana's usual treatment of it. Here Santayana does not mention the genteel tradition as harbinger of the Intellect. But he implies its presence in a culture which educates American youth in religious and literary traditions which are far removed from their actual experience and, consequently, are easily forgotten in the world of practice. He gives clearer prescription in this essay than elsewhere for the creation of an indigenous culture by calling for a more appropriate and vital practical life, one which will suggest naturally its own potentialities for developing the human spirit. Thus Santayana assumes that the American Will can create its own conditions for living beyond the practical life and, in doing so, be more appreciative and understanding of the traditions which link it to the efforts of other civilizations which have become human.

The subsequent essays in this section discuss the condition of America as Santayana found it in tradition and practice. "Philosophy on the Bleachers" describes one of Santayana's favorite metaphors for that which is vital in the American Will—the athletic contest. But he is hesitant to license this Will as an easy solution

to the ills of America. Although it has potential, it is still indifferent to that potential; and, in Arnoldian terms, Santayana
defines this indifference in "What Is a Philistine?" "Shakespeare:
Made in America" continues the criticism of the Will in a vastly
more ironical mood, showing Santayana's capacity to see the
humor in the moral plight of a nation. In "Genteel American
Poetry" Santayana returns to the characteristic American Intellect, which he thought had failed to aid the American Will in its
development; and he lays to rest more effectively than in "The
Genteel Tradition in American Philosophy" any question that
gentility in American letters may be relevant to American life or
that it may yet have been supplanted by anything which was
relevant. One fear held by some Americans was that the Catholic
religion might fill the moral if not the cultural gap. And in "The
Alleged Catholic Danger" Santayana ironically asserts that
though such an event would stifle what is essentially modern, it
would be something the world could survive as it had done
before. And with full cognizance of its dangers, Santayana claims
for a life under the Catholic tradition more freedom and sympathy for developing what is purely human than life has under
Protestantism.

In the final two essays, Santayana turns his attention to those
Davids of culture who are bent on defeating both the Philistines
and the aesthetes. In "America's Young Radicals" Santayana
reiterates the need for a viable tradition arising out of practice.
He does not discover the seeds of that tradition among the
new Intelligentsia; for in their haste to denounce the present,
they have forgotten the past and the lessons it can teach them in
style and discipline. "Marginal Notes on *Civilization in the
United States*" restates the argument against the radicals. But
Santayana's response to the book which solidified the radical
position in America includes perhaps his most comprehensive
analysis of American life and letters. Nowhere else, either before
or after 1922, either in *Character and Opinion in the United
States* or in *The Last Puritan*, did Santayana so clearly present
his opinions of America. And the reason for his doing so is much
the same as that which elicited his remarks on the genteel tradition: he saw in the disgruntled authors of these essays a wrong-
headed attempt to rescue American culture from the Philistines
and the new-humanists; and he wanted to refuse his approval of

their methods, particularly since a number had been his own students. Here he asserts that attitude of mind and spirit which allowed him to remain an independent and perceptive commentator on America throughout his life. And at the conclusion of the essay he turns significantly to the subject of humor, which he feels to be the matrix of a healthy and free spirit. Santayana proves to be a modern in the most philosophical and critical sense. His American criticism anticipates a state of mind, the *animal ridens,* which characterizes the free but disciplined spirit in a practical but absurd world.

TRADITION AND PRACTICE

At a moment like this, when some of you stand on the very mountain-top of youth, your traditional education spread out on one side beneath you, on the other the prospect of practical life, and when the rest of us also stand there with you, in thought and by force of sympathy,—it might not be unnatural for some wise man, who had descended long since into the plains, if he were a practical man and something of a reformer, to speak to you in the following manner: "My young friends; you may think you have completed your education; you are mistaken; you are going to begin it. What you have hitherto learned is verbal and, even if true in its way, is not understood by you in its real or human value. The first thing you will have to do is to forget it all, and to learn the alphabet of hard fact, and the arithmetic of practical forces. Your character, if you have acquired a good one, will help you in the world; but your learning and your budding ideas will fade year by year, crowded out by a new wisdom which as yet you know nothing of."

It is in some such way that a man schooled in affairs might perhaps address you; but being nothing but an academic person

Santayana delivered this address at the Oberlin Commencement, 1904. It was published in *The Oberlin Alumni Magazine,* October, 1904.

myself I may be excused if I put the matter somewhat differently. Life, after all, is made up of all its periods and the world of all its activities; and youth, too, has its ultimate moments. College is a part of the world, containing in miniature almost all its problems, and the world, if we use it intelligently, is nothing but a second university, another school of friendship, labour, and thought. In this half-hour in which I have the privilege of addressing you, I should like to dwell on this affinity between education and life, between tradition and practice. There is naturally a close connection between receiving something important from society and the past and rendering back something useful to society and to the future. You have heard a thousand times the demand that education should be practical, that traditions should not be insisted on and kept alive artificially, when they have no further function in actual life. You have also heard a thousand times, I am sure, that a man's life should be one of service to the world, that he should measure his own success by the degree in which it enables him to help others. As I repeat these familiar maxims I may seem to be turning a discourse, which presumably ought to be festive, into a class-room lecture or a downright sermon. But perhaps if we put those two commonplaces together we may get a somewhat more speculative idea, one that may well serve to light up the double vista greeting us on this occasion. This idea is that while tradition is only valuable when it is helpful in practice, practice itself is only valuable when it is fertile in tradition—that is, when it helps to create or bring to light something ideal, which can be transmitted from man to man, and from generation to generation.

In the modern world, and especially in America, tradition and practice appear in an anomalous relation. Both exist; both are powerful and complicated; yet they are in a way separated. Tradition flourishes almost unchallenged in the mind, while practice concerns itself chiefly with things material. The historical ground for this anomaly is very clear: if we divide tradition into three great streams—the literary, the religious, and the scientific—only the last, the scientific or economic tradition, which is a short tradition as yet, is native to our society: the other two come to us from alien races and remote periods of history. They were vital elements in civilizations which as a whole are dead; and surviving, as they do, in ours, they have in them something abstract and adventitious; we have to learn them like a foreign tongue. They influence our life, rather than express it; they endure as traditions to which we may give ourselves up more or less heartily; but the more we do so the more we seem to withdraw from practice and suggestions, to the abstract mind and its traditional lore. Here are two most remarkable facts— anomalies if we compare them with what is the case in most nations, and what must be the case with humanity at large—that our literary models are in dead and foreign languages, and that our religion is one to which our ancestors had to be converted, and which we need to be instructed in. Neither tradition is native; neither flows inevitably and of itself from our contact with nature and the spontaneous reflections of our minds. Only the third great stream of tradition—the scientific and economic—has grown up in our race under conditions such as those we still live in; and accordingly this third tradition hardly seems such; it seems rather part and parcel of the constitution of things. But science is a tradition, as government is: and if you or I had to begin a survey of nature for ourselves we should never arrive at a hundredth part of the knowledge needed to invent and construct a steam-engine, or to have our lives insured.

All tradition might conceivably be native in this same way. When a child is born he begins at once to educate his senses; he learns by groping to spell the external world and to attach himself to whatever in it helps to awaken his instincts, and to satisfy them. He explores house and field; he makes experiments in social intercourse, establishing his firm little allegiances and enmities—to parents, playfellows, strangers, and dolls. If we could imagine him growing up quite independently, yet shielded from all dangers as yet too grave for him, he would soon have a poetry, a science, and a morality of his own. Fantastic as these would doubtless be in their form, they would all centre around actual experience and somehow express it: his life, practical and imaginative, would be all of a piece. So poets actually feel the world. Convention has little power over them, either to impress on them useful things for which they do not care, or to choke off their native insights. It was largely in this way that the Greeks, that childlike and self-taught people, worked out their myths and their science; so that both were beautiful and legitimate, and even true, in so far as experience could as yet avail to control them.

What happens to our children, what happened to ourselves, when we embarked in childhood on this great voyage of discovery? We were led aside—of course, to be instructed—but we were led aside into regions not contiguous to what we could see or appreciate; our souls were transplanted from their native soil and bidden to bear fruits of very singular and alien grafting. I suspect that much of what I have in mind may not have fallen to your lot in the same aggravated form in which it fell to mine. Your teachers have, in many ways, brought education nearer to experience; they have sought in kindergartens and in nature-studies, in manual and economic training, to develope what was present to your senses and lead up without break to activities which were to be yours in future. It is a merit of Protestant Christianity to solicit religion rather than to impose it. It knows how to mould creeds to moral feeling, as this changes its emphasis, and it strives to represent throughout an inner personal impulsion. But suppose that these reforms had not taken place—and at best they are only partial—what would have happened to the child when he went to school and began to absorb tradition? He would have been ushered into hearsay worlds, real perhaps in themselves, but coming to him in the guise of superfluous fictions. These reports may find his imagination more or less receptive; they may entice him, as fairy-tales do, and make him wish he might wake up some fine morning in the world they describe; but I am not sure that it is when they are most welcome that they are most beneficial. Suppose he hears, as I did in my boyhood—and very gladly too—that in this world which he had just begun to spell out and find his place in, there is nothing really important; that to be dissatisfied here is only what is to be expected, for he is a pilgrim and stranger; that the earth is a vale of tears; that close above it, accessible at every turn, there is a supernatural realm, where his true pleasures should live; that there he can have his real friends and his real conversations; that there all his fortunes are mysteriously prepared and will have their miraculous and incalculable issues; so that he begins to walk the earth with a certain incredulity, and to translate its facts, as he meets them, into his own mystical language, reading into them values directly contrary, possibly, to those which they ostensibly have. This new mystical life may offer a congenial fourth dimension for his fancy to spread in; in those supernatural vistas he may discover something kindly and good, a needful refuge from his impotence or loneliness in the real world. But what a struggle in his heart! What an oscillation there must be in his allegiance between this world, in which he cannot well play his part without taking it seriously, and the other world, which he has been drawn into by an incidental tradition! But this is only the beginning of his distraction; another tradition remains behind.

Scarcely, indeed, has he accustomed himself to his double life and learned to speak his two languages together in a way intelligible, at least to himself, when he is led into a third universe. He begins to study the history and literature, perhaps even the philosophy, of Greece and Rome. As most often happens, the boy is merely pestered with what to him is a blind labour, producing a formal sort of knowledge soon happily to be unloaded on an examination paper and forgotten: but if he is quick and imaginative, with some premonitions in him of what a pure humanity might be, he very likely feels attracted to those masterpieces, and falls in love with that civilization, ancient in date, but more than modern, where moral interests are concerned, by its enterprise and freedom. But these classic memories and suggestions cannot be connected in the student's mind either with his own experience or with his religious instruction. Those early heroes are not pictured as doing anything which he himself might do. Those poetic and rhetorical passions do not express his family life, his public duties, nor his private problems and destiny. All is a mere fairyland, a literary tradition about exotic and distant things, surely not uninteresting in themselves, eloquent, very likely, to his speculative mind, but out of all relation to his practical existence.

Such was not the situation out of which those masterpieces themselves first grew. They were the work of young people, like the American, but people who, unlike the American, had no conscious traditions reaching far behind their youth. They were native products, in every fibre expressions of human nature at first hand. Suppose a copy of Virgil, such as our school-children use, could reach the poet in whatever honourable limbo we may fancy his spirit to inhabit. Would he not be at a loss to understand how things could have come to such a pass among us that we should compel ourselves to study a dead language and to read hundreds of verses none of which can have a native ring in our ears? "Is it possible," he might ask, "that you pretend to form your taste and mind by reading poets in a foreign language? What profit can you find in so artificial an exercise? Is it that you value our religion? No. Rome and the world it conquered perished more than a thousand years ago, and the piety with which I tried to express, in myths which to you have lost all their sanctity, her origin and spirit, is not piety for you: it is archaeology. Have you, then, no poets of your own to recast my patriotism and wisdom, so dressed that you may relish them—for the high passion and dignity of my lines must have been lost with their music? One would think your nations to be without arts: yet if you were wholly barbarous, how could you know the value of culture or go to the extreme pains which so tortured and sterile an education must involve? We Romans, to be sure, used to study Greek; but it was then a living tongue, spoken widely in our own dominions: we had nurses and native masters to teach it to us; we learned to speak it glibly, and found it afterwards useful when we became praetors and proconsuls in the East. Besides, we and the Greeks were kindred peoples, with a similar religion and polity, which in many ways had been developed in Greece more perfectly than in Latium, so that to us Greek literature was something better than native and more truly appealing—it was ideal. But you, to my astonishment, seem to sacrifice for a glimpse of unattainable excellence, and philosophies which you cannot apply to your affairs, whatever comfort, strength, and solid religion a homely education might bring. The Gauls and Germans, the Iberians and Britons of my day, though rude and unhappy, had an honest, patriotic pride which I cannot discover in you. They despised our traditions, so long as they defied our arms. No one among them, unless he wished to flatter Rome and was at heart a traitor, would have given his sons my poems to read. How comes it that your peoples, who have nothing to fear from our power, are still enslaved by our minds?"

What could we say to Virgil if he spoke to us in this way (as in all seriousness I believe he would) and what apology could we offer for the fact that we still read him? We should have to explain to him the whole riddle of our history: we should have to confess that only our young scientific and economic tradition is the fruit of our own genius: that for high things in literature and religion we still lean upon antiquity, sometimes, as in religion, venturing to adapt that tradition to our needs, and seeking to apply it in practice, sometimes, as in literature, almost abandoning the attempt to continue what we accept from the past, but keeping that past mummified and lifeless, to be the object of a contemplation called philology. And when he protested again at such behavior on our part, and threatened to hurl the word barbarous at us once more, not for our science and machinery, which he would immensely respect, but for our philology and our dependence on dead tradition—we should have to add this further explanation. We do not cling to tradition because it is old; it is not the barbarian's conservatism that makes us worship something conventional apart from ideal uses which it may have had in our own day. No: it is our incapacity so to exhaust and digest experience for ourselves as to rediscover what is eternally true in those traditions, that in them which is still vital in the world. We are in too great haste to understand ourselves, hence we must take for self-expression, and as a substitute for a mastery of experience which we dare not attempt, the self-expression and mastery of ancient, calmer spirits: we must let them still speak for us, because they still speak for us better than we are able to speak for ourselves. Virgil would be less surprised that we puzzle over his pages, if he knew the character of our own literature. Even seen through a veil, his world is clearer and more beautiful than ours. Even disfigured by our pedantic approach to it, his mind seems so majestic, exquisite, and true, that we can find nothing better for a model. His verses, sputtered in a barbarous mouth, are still our standard of excellence: his country's ruins are our best type of greatness: his religion, though not sacred to us as to him, remains the mould of our fancy, without which thought would lose half its symbols and nature half her amenity.

If our traditions, then, are in any way burdensome, if we are obliged to lean on them too much, it is only because we have not learned to draw tradition enough from our own practice. It is because the present yields so little as yet to the spirit, that the spirit looks behind to those heroic nations which knew how to make all things pay tribute to the mind. It was a smaller world, a quieter world, perhaps, that they were able to master: it brought them, for that very reason, more quickly to ultimate things. And for that reason, too, it is not possible for us to profit by their dominion directly. The principle of it we can adopt and reapply: the solution they gave is, in its form, inapplicable to us. Therefore, when we adopt it literally, it is apt to remain in the region of mere words. This, as it seems to me, is the great defect of our traditional education: it is a verbal education. And this is not because the objects with which our literature deals—be it sacred or profane—were themselves empty: no thought is further from my mind than that. The subject matter in both cases was living, it was momentous, it was engrossing; so engrossing, momentous, and living, that it made up, in each case, a whole world, with its own morality and civilization, with its own complete philosophy. But as neither of those worlds is ours, the literatures that express them do not educate us for our own life. They annex something to it; but this something is apt to remain a dead letter, seeing that we should have to transport ourselves out of our age and clime, if we were really to accept it practically and intelligently.

And what happens? We agitate ourselves amid these influences for a few years, while our verbal education is going on; but graduation comes: the real and sunlit world beckons us to begin an education through action. This is the point you have reached to-day; and many of you, I am sure, without any conscious dissatisfaction with what has gone before, look forward to the change with a high emotion, with the sense of power now for the first time to be really exerted, and real forces now for the first time to be met. You are eager to be done with tradition: it is practice you feel that will free your souls. Such a premonition cannot well be deceptive. It may be frustrated by chance in one or another of you, for in the most brilliant victories many fall by the way; but it can hardly be frustrated on the whole for a race and a generation that feels it distinctly. Much less can it be frustrated in America, where an altogether unprecedented career is open to human effort. This country has had the privilege of beginning with all the advantages of tradition and with none of its trammels. The advantages were a seasoned moral character, a religion free from gross superstition, possessed of the various practical arts and crafts current in Europe, and an almost empty continent in the temperate zone. Under such conditions practice ought to yield fruit quickly, and not to be much misinterpreted by the traditions to which it gives rise. Such traditions have in fact arisen—first in politics, and industry. New and appropriate moulds have been given to political and industrial life which not only secure efficiency but which engross intellect and inspire emotion. American life, every one has heard, has extraordinary intensity; it goes at a great rate. This is not due, I should say, to any particular urgency in the object pursued. Other nations have more pressing motives to bestir themselves than America has: and it is observable that not all the new nations, in either hemisphere, are energetic. This energy can hardly spring either from unusually intolerable conditions which people wish to overcome, nor from unusually important objects which they wish to attain. It springs, I should venture to say, from the harmony which subsists between the task and the spirit, between the mind's vitality and the forms which, in America, political and industrial tradition has taken on. It is sometimes said that the ruling passion in America is the love of money. That seems to me a complete mistake. The ruling passion is the love of *business,* which is something quite different. The lover of money would be jealous of it; he would spend it carefully; he would study to get out of it the most he could. But the lover of business, when he is successful, does not much change his way of living; he does not think out what further advantages he can get out of his success. His joy is in that business itself and in its further operation, in making it greater and better organized and a mightier engine in the general life. The adventitious personal profit in it is the last thing he thinks of, the last thing he is skillful in bringing about; and the same zeal and intensity is applied in managing a college, or a public office, or a naval establishment, as is lavished on private business, for it is not a motive of personal gain that stimulates to such exertions. It is the absorbing, satisfying character of the activities themselves: it is the art, the happiness, the greatness of them. So that in beginning life in such a society, which has developed a native and vital tradition out of its practice, you have good reason to feel that your spirit will be freed, that you will begin to realize a part of what you are living for.

At the same time, these congenial and ideal activities into which you will pass—what is called business, in the widest sense of the word—will still fail to contain all that would be ideal and congenial, it will leave certain powers in you unexercised, powers which in college, perhaps, you once felt you possessed and had begun to exercise. Your business, even if it be the business of teaching or of managing a college, will, as things now stand, look chiefly to material results. The question will be how many buildings you can put up, how many graduates you can turn out, how many books you can publish, and how many athletic victories you can score. To gain material results of this sort is itself an ideal object: without a material basis nothing spiritual can exist, or can reach expression; but the material basis is a basis only, as the body is in personal life, and when that has been rendered vigorous and healthy, the question still remains what further functions you are to give to your soul. There is, as the ancients said, a vegetative soul: it was very profound in them to see that vegetation also is spiritual, and that to perfect material instruments is already to embody an ideal. But the vegetative soul, in man, is only a background and a potentiality: the moral and intellectual functions must be superposed upon it. Will your business life, as you are likely to find it, supply adequately these moral and intellectual functions? Will you never have to pause, as for a Sabbath, and turn a speculative eye upon regions distant and serene? Will you not long sometimes for a holiday in the country, for solitude, for abstraction; thinking in that way to revert to something deeper and higher than your ordinary thoughts? Probably you will: and it is then that at church or in your library or in the woods, you will call back those sacred and remote traditions into which you were initiated in your youth: you will feel the need of them, and sigh, perhaps, for their painted worlds. In that case one thing will be plain: the tradition grounded on your daily practice and embodied there—the scientific, economic, political tradition of our age—will not have sufficed for your daily life. You will need something more, and the question is how you are going to get it.

And at this point, in bringing my discourse to a head, there is one thought I would urge upon you. You will never solve the problem satisfactorily or in a stable manner, you will never contribute to a truly sacred human tradition, so long as you are content to append your higher ideals, like postscripts, to your life. I once had a friend who feeling that there might be something narrow in his profession of glass-blower, thought he would go to Europe, as he expressed it, to pick up culture in the galleries. He went; but I could observe no conspicuous culture sticking to him on his return, and he is now blowing glass without it. Even if he had acquired it, it would have been a private possession, that would have gone with him to his grave. Suppose instead he had staid at home and spent his savings in buying books about glass-ware, and making experiments in more beautiful and appropriate forms to be given to glasses and bowls; he would have become a really cultivated man, one whose conversation any one would have been glad to listen to, and he would have established a better tradition in his art, one that might have made a difference for generations. Many a man, to take another example, absorbed in business and carrying it on in total abstraction from human feeling, may be most affectionate at home: he makes up to himself there for the inhumanity which he shows to the world. To the world, however, he never makes it up. His affectionate feelings are his self-indulgence, his self-deception: out of his public practice there flows no sweeter or kindlier tradition. It is time, perhaps, that by way of exception some great employer should deny himself a home and a family, as the monks did; that he should live among his workmen, in sight of the factory, so that his humanity might have a chance to spread itself out there, to beautify the places where life is at white heat; and such an employer, when his friends asked him where he lived and what was his family, might point like a sort of a masculine Cornelia to the happier colony about him and say: "These are my children." The principle is the same which the Apostle expresses when he says that whether we eat or drink we should do it for the glory of God: and while a certain alternation and rhythm is necessary in human life, and we must intensify our religion at certain moments, giving it more marked expression on some days and on some occasions than on others, that is merely a physical necessity: it is not the ideal of religion that it should be a thing apart and an escapade, as it were, from existence. Nor is that the ideal of any art; yet there are some people so ill-educated that when they have something to say, say it in the most imperfect and bungling fashion, and then, when their matter is exhausted, put in a rhetorical peroration, by way of showing that they too can be eloquent if they choose. But they prove the opposite, for their mouthings are as little eloquent as their crudities were; since eloquence does not consist in displaying a vocabulary when there is nothing to say. Eloquence is rather the essential rounding out of a thought, as you bring clearly to light the facts and emotions that justify it. You cannot be eloquent unless you are intelligent, and if you seem so, it will be only to those who are unintelligent themselves. Eloquence and art, religion and kindness, do not flourish in water-tight compartments: there needs to be a vital circulation among them if any of them is really to live.

It would therefore be a mere expedient, a sop thrown to Cerberus, if you appended one or more ideal interests to your practical life. In so far as you do so, you merely chill your practice, making it vulgar, unfruitful in liberal traditions, while at the same time you keep your ideality visionary and thin. The remedy, which it will take centuries to make thoroughly efficacious, but which every one may apply in a measure for himself, is simply to deepen practical life, to make it express all its possible affinities, all its latent demands. Were that done, we should find ourselves in unexpected and spontaneous harmony with the traditions which we might seem to have disregarded. For those ancient and alien traditions have survived because they express, each in its language, something which has a meaning at all times, something essentially human. Had our humanity, under its own conditions, found a full expression, it would have repeated unawares those accepted truths. If we then read Virgil, having come round to him in the natural development of our interest for all things human, we should love him for celebrating so loyally things also interesting to us: agriculture, and its cosmic emotions; nationality, with its deep springs and sacred responsibilities. For that is what Virgil is, not a labyrinth of syntax and prosody. In the same way our religious traditions would recover their rights, in the measure in which we found them prophetic of our deepest necessities. All traditions have been founded on practice: in practice the most ideal of them regain their authority, when practice really deals with reality, and faces the world squarely, in the interests of the whole soul. To bring the whole soul to expression is what all civilization is after. We must therefore be patient, for the task is long; but the fields are always white for the harvest, and the yield cannot be insignificant when labourers go forth into the harvest with the high and diligent spirit which we divine in you.

PHILOSOPHY ON THE BLEACHERS

In this early summer there is always an answer ready for the man who asks you, "Why do you go to games, why do you waste your time upon the bleachers?" The balm of the air, the lazy shadows of the afternoon, when it is too warm for a walk and too early for dinner, the return of the slack tide between lectures and examinations—all form a situation in which the path of least resistance often leads to Holmes Field. But although these motives lie ready as an excuse, and we may find them plausible, there remains a truer and less expressible interest behind. Motives are always easy to assign, unless we wish to get at the real one. Those little hypocrisies of daily life by which we elude the evils of self-analysis can blind us to our most respectable feelings. We make ourselves cheap to make ourselves intelligible. How often, for instance, do people excuse themselves, as it were, for going to church; the music is so good, the parson such an old friend, the sermon so nearly a discourse of reason. Yet these evasions leave untouched the ultimate cause why churches exist and why people go to them—a cause not to be assigned without philosophy. And it seems to me that similarly in this phenomenon of athletics there is an underlying force, a power of human

---

This essay appeared in *The Harvard Monthly*, July, 1894.

nature, that commonly escapes us. We talk of the matter with a smile as of a fad or a frolic, a meaningless pastime to which serious things are in danger of being sacrificed. Towards the vague idea of these "serious things," which might upon inspection be reduced almost without a remainder to the getting of money, we assume an attitude of earnest concern, and we view the sudden irruption of the sporting spirit with alarm and deprecation, but without understanding. Yet some explanation of the monster might perhaps be given, and as I have here a few pages to fill and nothing of moment to communicate, I will allow my pen to wander in the same direction as my feet, for a little ramble in the athletic field.

If it is not mere indolence that brings the spectators to our games, neither is it the mere need of healthy exercise that brings the players. The least acquaintance with them or their spirit is enough to convince one of this truth; and yet both friends and enemies of athletics are sometimes found speaking of them as a means of health, as an exercise to keep the mind clear and the body fit for work. That is a function which belongs rather to gymnastics, although the training for games may incidentally accomplish it. If health was alone or chiefly pursued, why should we not be satisfied with some chest-weights in our bedroom, a walk, or a ride, or a little swimming in summer? What could be gained by organized teams, traditional rivalries, or great contests where much money is spent and some bones possibly broken? It is amusing to hear people who are friendly to athletics by instinct or associations labouring to justify them on this ground. However much one may love buoyancy and generosity, and hate a pinched and sordid mind, one cannot help yielding the victory to the enemy when the battle is waged upon this utilitarian ground. Even arguments like those which the *New York Nation,* a paper often so intelligent, propounded not long ago on the subject of foot-ball, might then seem relevant, and if relevant conclusive. We should be led to believe that since athletics outrun the sphere of gymnastics, they have no sphere at all. The question why, then, they have come to exist would then pertinently occur, and might lead to unexpected results; but it is a question which the *Nation* and those of like mind need not answer, since to be silent is an ancient privilege of man of which the wise often avail themselves.

Now athletics have a higher function than gymnastics and a deeper basis than utility. They are a response to a natural impulse and exist only as an end in themselves. That is the reason why they have a kind of nobility which the public is quick to recognise, and why "professionalism" is so fatal to them. Professionalism introduces an alien and mercenary motive; but the valetudinarian motive is no less alien, and only harmless because so limited in scope. When the French, for instance shocked at the feeble health and ugliness of their school-boys, send commissioners to England and America to study athletics and the possibility of introducing them into France, the visitors return horrified at the brutality of Anglo-Saxon youth, and recommend some placid kind of foot-ball or some delightful form of non-competitive rowing, as offering all the advantages of fresh air and exercise, without the dangers and false excitements of the English practices. Any gymnastics, with or without pink tights, the French may easily introduce; they are no whit inferior to other nations in this field, as the professional circus can testify. But to introduce athletics into France there must be more than a change of ministry; there would have to be a change of ancestry. For such things are in the blood, and the taste and capacity for them must be inborn or developed by national experiences.

From a certain point of view we may blame athletic enthusiasm as irrational. The athletic temper is indeed not particularly Athenian, not vivacious, sensitive, or intelligent. It is rather Spartan, active, courageous, capable of serious enthusiasm and more ready to endure discipline than to ask for an ultimate reason for that devotion. But this reproach or irrationality ultimately falls upon every human interest, since all in the last analysis rest upon an instinct and not upon a rational necessity. Among the Greeks, to be sure, games had a certain relation to war; some of the contests were with weapons, and all were valued for developing martial qualities of soul and body. The relation of athletics to war is intimate, but it is not one of means to end, but more intrinsic, like that of the drama to life. It was not the utility of athletics for war that supported the Greek games; on the contrary, the games arose from the comparative freedom from war, and the consequent liberation of martial energy from the stimulus of necessity, and the expression of it in beautiful and spectacular forms. A certain analogy to war, a certain semblance of dire struggle, are therefore of the essence of athletics. Like war, they demand an organization of activities for the sake of victory. But here the victory is not sought for the sake of any further advantage. There is nothing to conquer or defend except the honour of success. War can thus become a luxury and flower into artistic forms, whenever the circumstances of life no longer drain all the energy native to the character. For this reason athletics flourish only among nations that are comparatively young, free, and safe, like the Greek towns and those American and Australian communities which, in athletics as distinguished from private sport, bid fair to outdo their mother country.

The essential distinction between athletics and gymnastics may help us to understand some other characteristics of our sports. They must, for instance, be confined to a few. Where so much time, skill and endurance are required, as in great athletic contests, the majority is necessarily excluded. If we were dealing with an instrument of health, a safety-valve or balance wheel to an overstrained system, the existence of an athletic aristocracy would be an anomaly. But the case is otherwise. We are dealing with an art in which only the few, the exceptionally gifted, can worthily succeed. Nature must be propitious, circumstances must be favourable, patience and inspiration must not fail. There is an athletic aristocracy for the same reason that there is one of intelligence and one of fashion, because men have different endowments, and only a few can do each thing as well as it is capable of being done. Equality in these respects would mean total absence of excellence. The analogy of moral and practical things would mislead us in this sphere. Comfort or happiness would seem to lose nothing of their value if they were subdivided, and a proportional fraction given to each individual: such an equal distribution of them might even seem a gain, since it would prevent envy, and satisfy a certain sense of mathematical justice. But the opposite happens in the arts. The value of talent, the beauty and dignity of positive achievements, depend on the height reached, and not on the number that reach it. Only the supreme is interesting: the rest has value only as leading to it or reflecting it. Still, although the achievement is rare, the benefit of it is diffused; we all participate through the imagination in the delight and meaning of what lies beyond our power of accomplishment. A few moments of enjoyment and intuition, scattered throughout our lives, are what lift the whole of it from vulgarity. They form a background of comparison, a standard of values, and a magnet for the estimation of tendencies, without which all our thought would be perfunctory and dull. Enthroned in those best moments, art, religion, love, and the other powers of the imagination, govern our character, and silently direct the current of our common thoughts.

Now, in its sphere, athletic sport has a parallel function. A man whose enthusiasm it has stirred in youth, has one more chamber in his memory, one more approach to things, and a manlier standard of pleasures and pains. An interesting task for somebody with adequate knowledge of antiquity would be to trace the influence which athletics had among the Greeks; I fancy it might be shown to permeate their poetry, to dominate their sculpture, and strangely to colour their sentiment. And this influence would come not chiefly from the practice but from the spectacle of games, just as the supposed brutalizing tendency of bull fighting is not conceived to stop with the performers within the ring, but to cross the barrier and infect the nation. Athletic sports are not children's games; they are public spectacles in which young men, carefully trained and disciplined, contend with one another in feats of strength, skill, and courage. Spectators are indispensable, since without them the victory, which should be the only reward, would lose half its power. For as Pindar, who knew, tells us:

> Success
> Is half the prize, the other half renown.
> Who both achieves, he hath the perfect crown.

A circumstance which somewhat perplexes this whole matter is the prevalent notion that athletics have a necessary relation to colleges. They have, indeed, a necessary relation to youth, because the time of greatest physical pliability and alertness is soon over; and as those of our youth who unite leisure with spirit are generally at some university, it happens that universities and colleges have become the centres of athletic interest. But this is an accident; a military or local organization of any sort would be as natural an athletic unit as a college. That athletic teams should bear the name of an institution of learning, and materially influence its reputation and fortune, is at first sight very strange; but the explanation is not far to seek. The English academic tradition, founded upon the clerical life of the middle ages, has always maintained a broad conception of education. All that an aristocratic family might wish to provide for its boys, that the schools and colleges provided. They contained the student's whole life, and they allowed a free and just development to all his faculties. The masters' province did not stop in the schoolroom, nor the professors' in the lecture hall. When possible they shared in the social and athletic life of the boys, and when not possible they at least gave it their heartiest support, making every reasonable concession to it; or, rather, not feeling that such friendliness was a concession at all, since they did not undertake merely the verbal education of their pupils, but had as broad an interest in their pursuits as the pupils themselves, or their parents. I remember a master at Eton, a man of fifty and a clergyman, running along the towpath in a sweater to watch the eight, a thing considered in no way singular or beneath his dignity. On the same principle, and on that principle alone, religious teaching and worship fall within the sphere of a college. To this system is due that beauty, individuality, and wealth of associations which make English colleges so beloved and venerable. They have a value which cannot be compensated or represented by any lists of courses or catalogues of libraries,—the value of a rounded and traditional life.

But even in England this state of things is disappearing. If we renounce it in this country, we need not suffer a permanent loss, provided the interests which are dropped by the colleges find some other social embodiment. Such a division of functions might even conduce to the efficiency of each; as is observed in the case of the German universities which, as compared with the English, are more active in investigation and more purely scientific in spirit, precisely because they have a more abstract function and minister to but one side of the mind. The real loss would come if a merely scientific and technical training were to pass for a human one, and a liberal education were conceived to be possible without leisure, or a generous life without any of those fruits of leisure of which athletics are one. Plato, who was beginning to turn his back upon paganism and held the un-Greek doctrine that the body should be cultivated only for the sake of the mind, nevertheless assigns in his scheme of education seven years to the teacher of the arts and seven to the athletic trainer.

This equality, I fancy, would seem to us improper only because the study and cultivation of bodily life is yet a new thing among us. Physically we are barbarians, as is proved by our clothes, our furniture, and our appearance. To bathe was not Christian before this century. But the ascetic prejudice which survives in some of our habits no longer governs our deliberate judgments. Whatever functions, then, we may wish our colleges to have we shall not frown long upon athletic practices altogether. The incoherences of our educational policy cannot permanently alter our social conditions or destroy the basis which athletics have in the instincts of the people.

Into physical discipline, however, a great deal can enter that is not athletics. There are many sports that have nothing competitive in them. Some of them, like angling, involve enough of mild excitement and of intercourse with nature to furnish good entertainment to the lovers of them, although not enough to amuse a looker-on. The reason is that angling is too easy; it requires, no doubt, a certain skill, but the effort is not visible and glorious enough, it has no relation to martial or strenuous qualities. The distinction between athletics and private sport is that between an art and an amusement. The possibility of vicarious interest in the one and its impossibility in the other are grounded on the meaning which athletics have, on their appeal to the imagination. There is in them a great and continuous endeavour, a representation of all the primitive virtues and fundamental gifts of man. The conditions alone are artificial, and when well combined are even better than any natural conditions for the enacting of this sort of physical drama, a drama in which all moral and emotional interests are in a manner involved. For in real life the latter are actually superposed upon physical struggles. Intelligence and virtue are weapons in life, powers that make, as our Darwinian philosophy has it, for survival; science is a plan of campaign and poetry a cry of battle, sometimes of one who cheers us on, sometimes of one who is wounded. Therefore, when some well-conceived contest, like our foot-ball, displays the dramatic essence of physical conflict, we watch it with an interest which no gymnastic feat, no vulgar tricks of the circus or of legerdemain, can ever arouse. The whole soul is stirred by a spectacle that represents the basis of its life.

But besides the meaning which athletic games may have as

physical dramas, they are capable, like other tragedies, of a great aesthetic development. This development they have not had in modern times, but we have only to conceive a scene at Olympia, or in a Roman amphitheatre, to see what immense possibilities lie in this direction. Our own games, in which no attention is paid to the aesthetic side, are themselves full of unconscious effects, which a practiced eye watches with delight. The public, however, is not sufficiently trained, nor the sports sufficiently developed, for this merit to be conspicuous. Such as it is, however, it contributes to our interest and helps to draw us to the games.

The chief claim which athletics make upon our respect remains yet unmentioned. They unite vitality with disinterestedness. The curse of our time is industrial supremacy, the sacrifice of every spontaneous faculty and liberal art to the demands of an over-grown material civilization. Our labour is servile and our play frivolous. Religion has long tended to change from a consolation into a puzzle, and to substitute unnatural checks for supernatural guidance. Art sometimes becomes an imposition, too; instead of delight and entertainment, it brings us the awful duty of culture. Our Muse, like Donna Inez, makes

> Her thoughts a theorem, her words a problem,
> As if she deemed that mystery would ennoble 'em.

One cannot read verse without hard thought and a dictionary. This irksome and cumbrous manner in the arts is probably an indirect effect of the too great prevalence of practical interests. We carry over into our play the principles of labour. When the stress of life and the niggardliness of nature relax a little and we find it possible for a moment to live as we will, we find ourselves helpless. We cannot comprehend our opportunity, and like the prisoner of Chillon we regain our freedom with a sigh. The saddest effect of moral servitude is this atrophy of the sponta-neous and imaginative will. We grow so accustomed to hard conditions that they seem necessary to us, and their absence inconceivable, so that religion, poetry, and the arts, which are the forms in which the soul asserts its independence, languish inwardly in the midst of the peace and riches that should foster them most. We have regained political and religious liberty, but moral freedom—the faculty and privilege of each man under the laws to live and act according to his inward nature—we scarcely care to have. The result is that while, in Greece, Sparta could exist beside Athens, Socrates beside Alcibiades, and Diogenes beside Alexander, we have in the United States seventy millions of people seized with the desire of absolutely resembling one another in dress, speech, habits, and dignities, and not one great or original man among them, except, perhaps, Mr. Edison.

It may seem a ridiculous thing, and yet I think it true, that our athletic life is the most conspicuous and promising rebellion against this industrial tyranny. We elude Mammon only for a few years, which the Philistines think are wasted. We succumb to him soon after leaving college. We sell our birthright for a mess of pottage, and the ancestral garden of the mind for building lots. That garden too often runs to seed, even if we choose a liberal profession, and is overgrown with the thistles of a trivial and narrow scholarship. But while we are young, and as yet amount to nothing, we retain the privilege of infinite potentiality. The poor actuality has not yet taken its place, and in giving one thing made everything else for ever unattainable. But in youth the intellectual part is too immature to bear much fruit; that would come later if the freedom could be retained. The body alone has reached perfection, and very naturally the physical life is what tends to occupy the interval of leisure with its exuberances. Such is the origin of our athletics. Their chief value is that they are the first fruits of that spontaneous life, of which the higher manifestations are not suffered to appear. Perhaps it is well that the body should take the lead, since that is the true and safe order of nature. The rest, if it comes, will then rest on a sounder basis.

When I hear, therefore, the cheering at our great games, when I watch, at Springfield or at New London, the frenzy of joy of the thousands upon one side and the grim and pathetic silence of the thousands upon the other, I cannot feel that the passion is excessive. It might seem so if we think only of what occurs at the moment. But would the game or the race as such be capable of arousing that enthusiasm? Is there not some pent-up energy in us, some thirst for enjoyment and for self-expression, some inward rebellion against a sordid environment, which here finds inarticulate expression? Is not the same force ready to bring us into other arenas, in which, as in those of Greece, honour should come not only to strength, swiftness, and beauty, but to every high gift and inspiration? Such a hope is almost justified by my athletic philosophy, which, with little else, perhaps, to recommend it, I here-with submit to the gentle reader. It may help him, if he receives it kindly, to fill up the waits at a game, while the captains wrangle, and to see in fancy greener fields than Holmes's from the bleachers.

WHAT IS A PHILISTINE?

If you live in Cambridge, dear Reader, or even in Boston, you may think the word Philistine is necessarily a term of reproach. It is, you may say, a synonym for the not-ourselves. Yet if this were so, and the word meant nothing but what is disliked by the speaker, the vast majority that lives elsewhere, in Seattle or in New York, would use it in turn to designate us, the eccentric minority. But it is notorious that they do not. They may call us dilettanti, Anglomaniacs, snobs, Unitarians, or "damn literary fellows"; they never call us Philistines. This term is not, then, like the word foreign, which means whatever is strange and unintelligible to us, whoever we are; it is rather like the word Irish or Mugwump, which signifies what is opposed or distasteful only to a certain tribe or fellowship of men. Such terms are essentially merely descriptive and geographical. Even Prussian is not necessarily a term of abuse; any one except a Frenchman might use it simply to denote a fact of civil allegiance, and to the ears of a corporal or a school-master it might even have a glorious sound. And so it might be with the word Philistine, were it not as yet too modern and metaphorical to be used by those to whom it applies, who, being of a somewhat conservative and plebian turn of mind,

---

This essay appeared in *The Harvard Monthly,* May, 1892.

prefer to call themselves "smart" fellows and "bright" girls. But if
any of them should do me the honor to read my definition of the
ancient and populous Philistine nation, they may henceforth
point with pride (as they are apt to do) to its glories as to their
own, and be as happy in being Philistines as they are now in
being Americans. Who knows if even you, dear Reader, inhabitant of Cambridge or Boston as you are, may not recognize
yourself in my description? Be not hasty, therefore, in condemn-
ing the Philistine: haply he is all that you most admire and
respect. But even if you are sure that the Philistine is horrid and
vulgar, I pray you to be patient with him for a while. I will try to
be so myself, for I too secretly dislike the Philistine; but we must
forget our tastes for a time, while, happy in the consciousness of
our silent sympathy, we proceed to describe the anatomy of the
creature as impartially and scientifically as we can. There is such
a thing as the Philistine in the economy of nature, and he has, as
Emerson would say, as much right to be as Cape Cod or Monad-
nock. He is a common, an impressive, almost a magnificent
phenomenon. He comprises, as we shall see, the greater part of
the reading and writing world. And our business is not now to
abuse him—except incidentally. Our task is to define him, a task
more worthy of our own liberal temper. A slight ebullition of
humors in the system is enough to inspire the most eloquent
invective, but to produce a tolerable definition of any category of
mortals requires all the resources of science and reflection.

We first hear of the Philistines in the Bible. They seem to have
lived by the sea, a thing not generally favorable to Philistinism.
There is a spiritualizing influence in the expanse of waters, which
carries the eye and the imagination at once to the clear horizon,
and tempts the sailor and the merchant beyond it. Voyaging
teaches us comparison, and, by revealing the many diversities of
life which are possible in this circumnavigable world, breeds a
certain noble humility founded upon self-knowledge, and a
certain tender and pathetic patriotism, which is not so much
a repulsion for the alien as a returning love for the peaceful,
comfortable, and familiar. For there are two stages in patriotism
as there are two in love. In the first we are proud of our country
or our mistress for what we deem her superlative beauties and
unrivalled virtues; in the second, we prefer her to all those who
outshine her, simply because she is our own. This is the way

Nature has of reconciling us to our necessary limitations, first by the blindness of passion, and afterwards by the power of habit.

But whether it was the unfavorable nearness of the sea, or the prowess of the heroes who judged Israel in those days, the ancient Philistines seem to have been less stubborn than the modern. The jawbone of an ass was then an efficient weapon against them, while now they can scarcely be mollified by all the honey that flows from the mouth of our young lions. It sufficed that a beautiful poet, a pastoral king, should defy their armies for the Philistines of those days to perish by the thousands and the ten thousands. How different it is now! Imagine the champion of our latter-day Philistia, Goliath become the spirit of some great corporation, to come forth with taunts before the army of the chosen people. And imagine some youthful saint, fresh from the unpolluted hills, and confident in the power of reason, to accept the challenge, and say, "Thou comest armed with the weight of five thousand shekels of brass, with a weaver's beam for a spear, pointed with six hundred shekels of iron, and one bearing a volume of Political Economy goes before thee; but I come to thee in the name of the Lord of Beauty, of the God of true and inward Happiness, whom thou hast defied. This day will the Lord deliver thee into my hand, and I will smite thee and take the souls of men away from thee: and I will give the high chimneys of the factories of the Philistines to the fowls of the air, and their deep furnaces to the beasts of the earth, that all the world may know that there is a God in Israel." Would our intrepid David, after all this bold language, find any smooth stones in the brook, or have any skill with the sling, to smite the forehead of that Goliath? I am afraid the assembly would have reason to laugh at him, and to remain convinced that, in our day at least, it is with the sword and the spear that the Lord saveth.

The Bible tells us no more about the Philistines. We need not wonder at it, for such a beautiful apparition as David was capable, if anything ever was, of making an end of them. And shamed, as it were, by his life and his song, Philistia disappeared from the earth for several thousand years, to reappear at last in modern Germany. For although the modern Philistine is not necessarily Teutonic, yet it was the German imagination and learning that first noted the similarity between certain elements of modern society and the ancient enemies of Samson and David.

In those idyllic days when the Fatherland was happy with the empire of the air, the German student, tender, unpolitical stripling that he was, delighted to quaff his beer and ogle his lass under the trellises of a rural inn, or to sit all night in the vaulted *Rathskeller* of his university town, where his idealistic soul glowed with genial enthusiasm, and the ruddy image of Gambrinus, astride upon a barrel, leered at him from the painted wall. As his imagination kindled with the fumes of the malt mingled with the inspirations of genius, he saw in his expanding consciousness the fulfilment of the law and the prophets. And when he was awakened at last by the necessity, perhaps, of paying his bill, he spontaneously gave to his fleshly and unsympathetic host the name of *Philister,* as being his natural enemy, and the chief earthly obstacle to the infinite fulfilment of his dreams.

From the blameless inn-keeper, who doubtless understood nothing of the student's cant, the epithet was extended to all shop-keepers, towns-men and merchants, until we hear Heine dividing the population of Göttingen into students, professors, Philistines, and kine. These classes, he is careful to add, are not mutually exclusive; but even with this qualification his classification is now out of date. No one would think of drawing a distinction now-a-days between the Philistines and the professors of Germany. The ordinary German professor is, with the possible exception of the German parson, the most contented dweller in Philistia Felix. Full of reverence for the state of which he is the organ, and for the lexicons and monographs which he devours and brings forth with physiological regularity, he rejoices in the consciousness of being a normal and well-regulated cell in the organism of modern society and of modern science. If you asked him what he or any other cell gained thereby, he would look upon you with astonishment, and reply: My living! How should it be an expense of spirit in a waste of shame to write dull and unnecessary books, when these enlarge the "literature" of science and are placed upon the shelves of libraries? And as for the student, with his *Notizen* and his hourly odoriferous slice of sour *Butterbrod;* of what are his dreams but of a *Kneipe* or a degree, a low debauch or an *ordentliche Professur?* Both masters and pupils are excellent examples of that unquestioning subordination of mind to matter and of ends to means which is the essence of Philistinism.

If Heine could now revisit his native country the class that he would contrast with Philistines would be musicians. They alone, with a small retinue of painters and poets, and other lovers of decaying arts, constitute Bohemia, and inherit the spiritual freedom of the former student. Music is the most exclusively aesthetic and unutilitarian of the arts, and by a sort of sarcasm of fate, or by the tendency of a restless and disorganized society to run into extremes, is the one now most passionately and successfully pursued. The musician lives, if not by ideas, at least by emotions, and in his enthusiasm for beauty, in his capacity for rapture, in his unfettered life, he shows the blithe spirit of an angel, too often combined, alas! with the habits of a pig. For musical susceptibility is a thing by itself, easily separable from every other element of culture; and in this fact we have, perhaps, the true cause of the present preëminence of music, since the less beauty we are able to see in external things the more we fall back upon the pure beauty of sensation. But cultivation in general and cleanliness in particular were never necessary to spirituality; and in spite of his unpleasant neglect of the body, the musician is all over the world, and especially in Germany where he most abounds, the champion of the soul, who like his patron the Psalmist defies the hosts of the Philistines.

It is in England, however, and in this country, that we are wont to think the Philistine most at home. Everybody knows Mr. Matthew Arnold's division of the English into barbarians, Philistines, and rabble, and also his subsequent remark that America is the paradise of Philistinism. It is obvious from these sayings, as well as from that of Heine already quoted, that the Philistines must be many and heterogeneous. They are not to be easily described except by exclusion; the other classes contrasted with them are all more definite and describable. For we all know what a musician is, and students and professors we have always with us. Kine and rabble are a distinct and well-known estate, happily not yet numerous in this New World. They are that species of animal which, although externally human, is without family, arts, or religion. And the barbarians we also know, or wish to, for they are the aristocracy. They are the country gentlemen and club

men, who hunt, cruise, shoot, bathe, dress, and go upon the
grand tour; men who love their horses, their hounds, their parks,
and their dinner, and who regard a poet and a scholar, like Mr.
Arnold, as something intermediate between a pedagogue and a
comedian,—a subtle person fed and clothed at the expense of
society for the delight and amusement of the lords of the earth.
And the men of culture—a class too insignificant in numbers to
be included in the general division—are such as Mr. Arnold
himself, and occupy in England the place held by the musicians
in Germany. The Englishman is of course immensely superior in
civilization, but he lives in a society grossly barbarian, and
catches some of the traits of the ruling caste; he washes and he
dines at eight o'clock, and he is not wholly without snobbery.

All these various classes of the non-Philistine are comparatively
easy to recognize and to define roughly. But what characteristics
shall we say are distinctive of the vast remainder, which by
common consent we call the Philistines? Well, we may begin by
saying without much fear of contradiction that one essential trait
of the Philistine is conventionality. We have all heard that the
English middle class is eminent for dullness and stupidity. The
English Philistine is a man of narrow, wholly practical interests,
rigid and verbal principles, stubborn contempt for what is alien
or new, and not less dogged attachment to what is authoritative
and homespun. But this description does not apply to the emancipated middle class: it does not at all apply to the American,
who is also a Philistine. The conventionality we mean must be
carefully distinguished from Toryism. To be a Tory is at least to
have affections and prejudices which in their very irrationality
seem to have something un-Philistine about them. Toryism is an
instinctive if not a reasoned avowal of the value of a social ideal;
it is attachment to the hierarchy in church and state, and to the
rural life of England. To get Philistinism pure and unalloyed we
must turn to the prosperous shop-keepers and merchants who
dwell in towns, compared with whom your country Tory is a
figure of romance. For the prosperous business man, who is a
radical, has prejudices without affections, and his thoughts are
governed by insistence on a doctrine rather than by loyalty to an
institution. His mind is empty without being free. And it is, I
should say, of the essence of the Philistine mind to have rigidity
without substance. However narrow a life may be, however

ignorant of the wide world of nature and thought, if it is governed by some true perception, if it has hold upon some immediate and vital good, it escapes conventionality. For that reason neither a saint nor a voluptuary can be a Philistine; they know too well what they are living for, and its intrinsic worth. Nor was that woman a Philistine whom Sir Edwin Arnold makes to say:

> "My heart
> Is little, and a little rain will fill
> The lily's cup that hardly moists the field.
> It is enough for me to feel life's sun
> Shine in my Lord's grace and my baby's smile.
> Pleasant my days pass, filled with household cares
> From sunrise when I wake to praise the gods
> And set my housemaids to their tasks, till noon
> When my Lord lays his head upon my lap
> Lulled by soft songs and wavings of the fan.
> And so to supper time at quiet eve
> When by his side I stand and serve the cakes.
> But if death called Senani, I should mount
> The pile, and lay that dear head in my lap
> My daily way, rejoicing when the torch
> Lit the quick flame and rolled the choking smoke.
> For it is written if an Indian wife
> Die so, her love shall give her husband's soul
> For every hair upon her head a crore
> Of years in Swerga. Therefore fear I not."

Such a woman would hardly have been what we call a woman of culture; she would not have enjoyed Wordsworth or Ruskin even in a translation. But it is her quiet indifference to both translations and originals, her perception of the primary things in life, and her repose in them, that makes her noble. No one who leads the simple life of the senses and the affections can be called a Philistine. To reach that condition there must supervene a certain sophistication, and the mind must lose its perception of primitive facts in its attention to conventional maxims. Philistinism is life at second hand.

Nothing, for instance, is so Philistine as the habit of asking the money value of everything, and of talking, as our newspapers do, of a thousand-dollar diamond and a ten-thousand-dollar fire. A man whose eye was single would tell you how much the one sparkled and the other blazed. But the Philistine's senses are muffled by his intellect and by his habit of abbreviated thinking.

His mental process is all algebra, a reckoning that loses sight of its original values and is over without reaching any concrete result. Now the price of an object is an algebraic symbol; it is an abstract term, invented to facilitate our operations, which remains arid and unmeaning if we stop with it and forget to translate it again at the end into its concrete equivalent. It is vulgar to esteem things for their cost, but not vulgar to esteem them for the qualities which make them costly. I believe the economists count among the elements of the value of an object the rarity of its material, the labor of its manufacture, and the distance of the country from which it is brought. Now all these qualities, if attended to in themselves, appeal greatly to the imagination. We have a natural interest in what is rare and affects us with unusual sensations. What comes from a far country carries our thoughts there, and gains by the wealth and picturesqueness of its associations. And that on which human labor has been spent, especially if it was a labor of love and is apparent in the product, has one of the deepest possible claims to admiration. So that the standard of cost, the most vulgar and Philistine of all standards, is such only when it remains empty and abstract. Let the thoughts wander back and consider the elements of value, and our appreciation, from being verbal and commercial, becomes real and poetic.

One characteristic of the Philistine mind, then, is its resting in the merely conventional. It is in a hurry and deals in abbreviations. Dexterity in the use of symbols and respect for the instruments of calculation make it forget the vision of the real world and the primitive source of all value in the senses and the affections. It used to be a doctrine of philosophers that the world was made for man and everything in it designed for his comfort and salvation. That belief is now impugned, and people think that the universe may have other purposes, if it has any purpose at all, than one which is so disproportionate to its extent and which it is so slow in accomplishing. But I know not whether it is on account of this new philosophy, or on account of ancient habits and practical impulses, that we have got into a way of living as if not only the aim of Nature, but also the aim of man and of society, lay beyond man himself. We have multiplied our instruments, and forgotten our purposes; and, what is still worse, we have made of ourselves instruments for the production of

changes in Nature, and consented to regard our consciousness as
a device for the better making and doing of things. We have
forgotten that there is nothing valuable or worthy in the motion,
however rapid, of masses, however great, nor in the accumulation
of objects, however numerous and complicated, nor in the organization of societies, however great and powerful, unless the
inward happiness of men is thereby increased or their misery
diminished. This idolatry, that subordinates the life of man, his
thoughts and his actions, to the production of external effects in
the world, is the religion of Philistia; and nothing so much
arouses the inspired rage of the true prophet; witness the cry of
Leopardi:

> Age in which I was born,
> Thou fool that, heaping treasure for the morrow,
> Unto each sad today but addest sorrow,
> I hold thy pride in scorn!

But if blindness to the elemental and immediate is one condition of Philistinism, indifference to the supreme and ultimate is
another. Our Indian woman not only perceives the intrinsic
sufficiency of simple joys, she also conceives of a highest duty
and consolation, she forms an idea of her place in the universe,
and has a religion. Now a Philistine may be very religious in his
gregarious way, his faith may be orthodox and his conduct irre-
proachable. But he would cease to be a Philistine if he had
instinctive piety and an inward, imaginative appreciation of his
faith. For these things require a certain wealth of emotion and
scope of imagination; they involve what we call unworldliness. To
be unworldly is to look upon the judgment of society, its prizes
and its pleasures, with the serenity and sadness of one whose
treasure is elsewhere and whose eyes have beheld the vision of
better things. It is to live in the sight of the ideal,

> Ayant devant les yeux, sans cesse, nuit et jour,
> Ou quelque saint labeur ou quelque grand amour.[1]

It matters not what the sacred passion or what the work of love
may be: the infinite surrounds us in every direction, and all who
at any time have caught a glimpse of it have something in

---

[1] "Having before one's eyes, constantly, night and day, / Either some
saintly work or some great love."

common. They have for a moment escaped convention and felt the relativity and possible indifference of all earthly goods. That is what the Philistine has never done. He has never shaken off his vulgar passions nor felt the weight of original sin; his life, like that of a beast of burden, has not been either a revel or a sacrifice, but a stolid response to successive stimulations.

If this be the sad condition of the Philistine, we need hardly ask why he has another quality, which many people may think the most essential to him, namely, indifference to the beauties of art. For art appeals to the vividness of sensation and to the sweep of fancy; it charms by clearness of form and by infinity of suggestion. But we have seen how the Philistine can never repose in sense, since every sensation is to him merely a sign and symbol, a signal that something is to be done. And he is equally incapable of attaining to imagination, for what he sees and hears suggests to him facts, and facts in turn suggest to him nothing. So that if you set a Philistine before a picture, he will be inevitably bored. He can do nothing to the picture except buy it, and that is soon accomplished. He is too active and industrious a man to stand gaping at it, pretending he enjoys the harmony of its color, the balance of its design, or the richness of its light and shade. And he is too honest to say that the picture represents anything more than a man's face, or a pretty view, or whatever else the subject may be. If the reproduction is accurate, as far as his perception goes, he will be pleased to notice the fact. But how the image of a face can represent anything besides, or the copy of a landscape be more beautiful than the original, he can never conceive. The comprehension of that depends on the awakening of many dim and profound suggestions, on the creation in the beholder's mind of some ideal of beauty or of happiness, on the quick passing of some infinitely tragic and lovely vision. And such things are not engendered in the Philistine brain.

With this, dear Reader, I take my leave. If by my description you have found that you are a Philistine yourself, do not be too much troubled. I have said hard things of you, and I cannot retract them, for I believe them to be true. But I may add another, no less true, which may serve for your consolation. The time will come, astronomers and geologists assure us, when life will be extinct upon this weary planet. All the delights of sense and imagination of which I have been speaking will then be over.

But the masses of matter which you have transformed with your machinery, and carried from one place to another, will remain to bear witness of you. The collocation of atoms will never be what it would have been if your feet had less continually beaten the earth. You have the happiness of knowing that, when nothing I value endures, the earth may still sometimes, because of you, cast a slightly different shadow across the craters of the moon.

SHAKESPEARE: MADE IN AMERICA

Custom blinds us to the costume of thought. Not until the fashion has entirely changed do we see how extravagant the old costume was. The late middle ages and the renaissance, when modern languages took shape, had a very elaborate and modish dress for the mind as well as for the body. Notice, for instance, how Shakespeare can deck out a Hock sentiment, proper to any schoolboy:

> When in disgrace with fortune and men's eyes
> I all alone beweep my outcast state
> And trouble deaf heaven with my bootless cries
> And look upon myself and curse my fate,
> Wishing me like to one more rich in hope,
> Featur'd like him, like him with friends possess'd,
> Desiring this man's art and that man's scope,
> With what I most enjoy contented least,
> Yet in these thoughts myself almost despising,—
> Haply I think on thee; and then my state,
> Like to the lark at break of day arising
> From sullen earth, sings hymns at heaven's gate:
> For thy sweet love remember'd such wealth brings
> That then I scorn to change my state with kings.

This essay was published in *The New Republic,* February 27, 1915. It has been reprinted in *The New Republic Anthology, 1915: 1935,* edited by Groff Conklin, New York, 1936.

For Shakespeare this sonnet is comparatively plain and direct, yet it is simply encrusted with old-fashioned jewels and embroideries. How much so will become clear if we venture to paraphrase it, scrupulously leaving out every suggestion that could not have had its origin in the twentieth century and in America.

In the first few lines almost every connotation is obsolete and will have to be abandoned. So the idea of falling out of favor at a court where the capricious monarch is Fortune. This mythological Fortune was rather a verbal deity from the beginning and had become merely rhetorical even in Shakespeare's time; for us it is worse, and the unrepublican image is inadmissible. To *beweep* anything is also contrary to our manners; if tears ever escape us it is not ceremoniously nor as a fit accompaniment to magnificent lamentations. As to *men's eyes,* we look through our eyes, but seldom talk through them; and if we wish to shake off an objectionable friend we do not cast withering glances upon him, like the noble savage. We simply avoid the man; or if we are inclined to be offensively demonstrative, we cut him. The word *outcast* is still current; but the background which gave poignancy to that metaphor belongs to a by-gone age. No one can be easily excommunicated in our tolerant society. If one circle disowns him he will slip into another, perhaps with relief, and find it no less self-respecting, even in jail; and if he makes bold to flaunt his crime or his heresy, he will excite more interest than loathing, and a party of sympathizers will probably flock to his side.

No less obsolete is the habit of troubling heaven with one's bootless cries. Even the lover in the sonnet, though he might have prayed, would hardly have emitted cries; only in remote antiquity his predecessors in the art of troubling heaven may actually have wailed. Nowadays hardly anybody would pray in the hope of recovering his friends or his property by divine interposition. People certainly have recourse to religion, and often in a more desperate need than ever; but to modern feeling religion opens a second sphere of interest and hope, without being expected to further our worldly hopes and interests.

In the body of the sonnet there are a number of phrases which, without being in the least archaic, have a certain grand sweeping air and *panache* about them foreign to our experience. The word *art,* for instance, to most Americans suggests the profession of painting; the intended faculty of doing all things easily and well would have to be called ability or skill, or more pungently and characteristically, *brains*. This single transition from art to brains speaks volumes. Again, while no nation was ever more hopeful than America or more optimistic, to say *rich in hope* is to give the matter a different twist. You are optimistic when you take for granted or religiously assure yourself that the future, whatever it may be, will be all right, and will somehow grow better and better. You are rich in hope when you have great and definite expectations, are heir or aspirant to an exalted position, and can picture in a concrete form the happy future before you. So a bridegroom is rich in hope on his wedding morning, or an expectant mother when making bibs for her first-born; but the optimist may be as poor in hope as in experience.

Similarly the phrase *I look upon myself* expresses something different from our self-consciousness. It describes the shock of suddenly seeing yourself as others see you, as when you unexpectedly come upon yourself in a mirror. The poet is borrowing men's eyes in order to consider and pity himself; he is not retreating into a psychological observation of what is hidden from others in his consciousness.

The eleventh and twelfth lines will have to be sacrificed in their entirety. There are no larks in America. There is no heaven in modern cosmology such that the blue sky in which larks sing should be called the gate of it. And what hymns could the poet have been thinking of? Christmas carols, perhaps, or such as the choir of Magdalen College in Oxford greet the sunrise with on May morning from the top of their lovely tower. In any case they were pre-Puritan hymns, hymns of joyful familiarity with a religion sweetly and humanly miraculous, hymns not associated with drawling tunes, funerals, or a vague sense of constraint and edification. For these two lines, therefore, we must substitute something wholly different, yet as nearly equivalent as possible. I can think of nothing domesticated in America nearer to larks and to bright religion than music is. So orchestral strains shall take the place of larks, with profound apologies; and in speaking of music we may perhaps slightly inflate the poetic bellows, since modern shyness does not attack our souls so much in that invisible wilderness.

As to the final couplet, we may still talk occasionally of being as happy as a king or as drunk as a lord, but whatever seduction there may once have been in those images, they have paled. Something of far greater moment, however, lies submerged here. The unsophisticated reader may pass approvingly over the phrase *thy sweet love,* as if the poet might just as well have written *our sweet love* instead, meaning that mutual, complete, hearty, happy, plebeian love which alone should figure in our revised American version. Yet as a matter of fact the sentiment and pathos of the original are profoundly different, being charged with the most exotic metaphysical overtones. If we compare this sonnet with the rest of Shakespeare's, and consider the W. H. to whom at least by a poetic fiction they were addressed, it becomes evident that *thy sweet love* can only mean *the sweet love of thee,* a love which the poet did not and could not aspire to see returned. That ornate and exuberant age had so much passion to spare that it could think it but grateful adulation for a poet to address the intensest and richest effusions of love to some insipid youth in a high station. And behind that lavish play of expression (for perhaps it was nothing more) we must not ignore the possibility that the passion expressed may sometimes have been real, at least in those who first set this literary fashion; and in that case, seeing that even if graciously tolerated, such adoration could not possibly be mutual, we are at once transported into the dim sanctuary of Platonic love, where youth and beauty, at an aesthetic remove and because of their intrinsic virtue, are reputed to communicate a sufficient bliss to the worshipper, with all those moral and saving effects which this sonnet, for instance, celebrates. The lover in his infatuation, and in the religious chastening of it, is said somehow to find God. Humbug or philosophy, this Platonic mysticism has long been a classic refuge of hopeless emotion, and Shakespeare's sonnets march conventionally in the devout procession. Such ambiguous mysteries, however, are alien to modern sentiment and to the plain man's experience, and we may shut them out without further parlance.

Plucked of all its Elizabethan feathers, our sonnet might then present somewhat the following appearance:

> When times are hard and old friends fall away
> And all alone I lose my hope and pluck,
> Doubting if God can hear me when I pray,
> And brood upon myself and curse my luck,
> Envying some stranger for his handsome face,
> His wit, his wealth, his chances, or his friends,

Desiring this man's brains and that man's place,
And vexed with all I have that makes amends,
Yet in these thoughts myself almost despising,—
By chance I think of you; and then my mind,
Like music from deep sullen murmurs rising
To peals and raptures, leaves the earth behind:
For if you care for me, what need I care
To own the world or be a millionaire?

The reader may laugh, but I have not made the sonnet absurd on purpose; on the contrary I have tried to keep it as good as possible under the conditions imposed. The experiment is not intended to show how an American poet would actually feel or treat Shakespeare's subject, for he would either compose fine imitative literature, with a lapse here and there which he might not be conscious of, or else he would give birth to something entirely novel. The experiment is meant only to make evident how much old finery there is in our literary baggage, and how original an original poet would have to be. Any wise man of Shakespeare's time might have prophesied that ruffs would no longer be worn in three hundred years, but only a genius could have foretold our trousers. So any critic may unfrock Shakespeare, but to dress his thought up again in the costume of a future poetry can be given only to the future poets themselves.

GENTEEL AMERICAN POETRY

Poetry in America before the Civil War was an honest and adequate phenomenon. It spoke without affectation in a language and style which it could take for granted. It was candid in its tastes, even in that frank and gentle romanticism which attached it to Evangelines and Maud Mullers. It modulated in obvious ways the honorable conventions of the society in which it arose. It was a simple, sweet, humane, Protestant literature, grandmotherly in that sedate spectacled wonder with which it gazed at this terrible world and said how beautiful and how interesting it all was.

The accent of these poets was necessarily provincial, their outlook and reflectiveness were universal enough. Their poetry was indeed without sensuous beauty, splendor, passion, or volume, but so was the life it expressed. To be a really great poet an American at that time would have had to be a rebel.

It would have been an interesting thing if a thunderclap had suddenly broken that cloudless new-world haying-weather, and if a cry of exasperation had escaped some strong soul, surfeited by the emptiness and blandness of that prim little moral circle that thought it had overcome everything when in fact it had

This essay was published in *The New Republic*, May 29, 1915.

touched nothing. But to the genteel mind of America, before
Walt Whitman and the Civil War, there was no self-respecting
opposition. Of course, in that boundless field of convention,
prosperity and mediocrity, a wild poppy might struggle up
weedily here and there amid the serried corn. But the irregular
genius had no chance. He felt sincerely ashamed of himself. He
hid his independence, fled to the back woods or to Europe, and
his sad case was hushed up as if it had been insanity (for insanity
was hushed up too) and buried with a whisper under the
vaguely terrible epitaph DISSIPATED. He probably died young;
at any rate he never "did" anything. Whoever was unharnessed
was lost.

In England at about the same time or earlier there was a
marked division between the poets who were national, conventional and edifying and those who were disaffected. Wordsworth
and Tennyson were more than matched by Byron, Shelley, and
Swinburne. What occasioned this division in England was the
very distinct and intolerant character of the national mind. You
either identified yourself with it and expressed it sympathetically,
or you broke away from it altogether, denounced it as narrow,
stupid, and oppressive, and removed yourself offendedly to
Greece or to Italy, to sing of lovely sensuality or celestial justice.
A circumstance that made such romantic truancy all the easier
for poets was the classical cast of their education. History, religion, and literary tradition, united with the ease of travel, carried
the mind of every educated man continually beyond the limits of
his country and its present ways. When one's moral possessions
are so largely of foreign extraction, it requires no break with one's
education, but merely a certain deepening and arrest in it, for
things not national to seem the right environment for the soul.
Exile accordingly did not sterilize the British poets: on the
contrary, it seemed to liberate their genius and carry them back,
across the Reformation, to an England as poetical if not so
vigorous as that of Shakespeare.

Why did not disaffected Americans figure among these poets
of the foreign, or rather of the human, ideal? The provocation to
secede was certainly not less than in England; for if the country
was not dominated by any church or aristocracy, it was dominated no less rigidly by democracy and commercialism. The land
was indeed broader, and those who felt spiritually restive could

without any great scandal make for the Wild West. This was certainly a resource for adventurous temperaments; but those whose impatience was moral, whose need was not so much for room as for something to fill it, could hardly be satisfied there; for morally all America even to-day is far more monotonous and uniform than England ever was. It was perhaps this very pressure of sameness which might have justified a poetic protest, that prevented it from arising.

The insurrection that actually took place was that of Walt Whitman, with the magnificent intention of being wholly direct, utterly sincere, and bothering about nothing that was not an experience of the soul and of the sense here in the motley foreground of life. It is notable that this powerful insurrection in favor of what is modern and national has made so little difference. Of course, nothing can compel people to read or to like an author that displeases them. Perhaps Walt Whitman made the mistake of supposing that what was vital in America was only what was absolutely modern and native, to the exclusion of anything that might have been transplanted to this country ready-made, like the Christian religion or the English language. He wished to be wholly impressionistic, wholly personal, wholly American, and the result was perhaps that he was simply mystical, missing the articulation of the great world, as well as the constructive mind of his own age and country. After all, the future often belongs to what has a past. Walt Whitman renounced old forms without achieving a new one, and in his thought also there was more detritus than invention.

At any rate, the genteel manner having become obsolete, and the manner of the great mystical tramp not having taken root, the poetic mind of America suffered a certain dispersion. It was solicited in turn by the seductive aesthetic school, by the influence of Browning, with his historico-dramatic obsessions, by symbolism, by the desperate determination to be expressive even with nothing to express, and by the resolve to write poetry which is not verse, so as to be sure of not writing verse which is not poetry. The spontaneous me has certainly been beaten in the first round by the artistic ego. Meantime the average human genteel person, with a heart, a morality, and a religion, who is after all in the majority, is left for the moment without any poetry to give him pleasure or to do him honor.

THE ALLEGED CATHOLIC DANGER

Alarm seems to be felt in various quarters about the power of the Catholic church in the United States. After being long obscure and tolerated with a smile, apparently the prelates are beginning to wear their robes in public and to boast that the future of religion in America is in their hands. This assurance is itself more American than Catholic. The tone prevalent in the church from the earlier ages has been (saving the eloquence) like that of the Hebrew prophets, one of lamentation, foreboding and invective; what is good is at best a consolation that may perhaps put off the evil day. But the tone of the American Catholics is pleasantly American. It is wonderful how silently, amicably, and happily they live in a community whose spirit is diametrically opposed to that of their religion.

Mr. John Jay Chapman in his "Notes on Religion" explained half of this anomaly. "We have not been interested in religion; we have forgotten the principles of the matter. The extraordinary ignorance of our people in matters of history, their belief in destiny, their inability to stop and reflect about anything, their desire that our politics shall not contain any religious question, their sense of security—all these things have led the Americans of

---

This essay was published in *The New Republic,* January 15, 1916.

the last fifty years to hide their heads in the sand in regard to the doings of the Roman Catholic Church." But the other half of the anomaly remains unexplained, how the Catholic faith, in persons who hold it so sincerely and affectionately as the Irish do, for instance, can leave them entirely at peace in a land where everything—traditions, government, manners, standards, and hopes—implies a profound disbelief in any such system.

American life is a powerful solvent. As it stamps the immigrant, almost before he can speak English, with an unmistakable muscular tension, cheery self-confidence and habitual challenge in the voice and eyes, so it seems to neutralize every intellectual element, however tough and alien it may be, and to fuse it in the native good-will, complacency, thoughtlessness, and optimism. The American Catholic looks at his inherited religion in this acquired spirit. His church, he feels, is a first-rate church to belong to; the priests are fine fellows, like the policemen; the Sisters are dear noble women, like his own sisters; his parish is flourishing, and always rebuilding its church and founding new schools, orphan asylums, sodalities, confraternities, perpetual adoration societies. No parish can raise so much money for any object, or if there are temporary troubles, the fact still remains that America has three Cardinals and that the Catholic religion is the biggest religion on earth. Attachment to his church in such a temper brings him into no serious conflict with his Protestant neighbors. They live and meet on common ground. Their respective religions pass among them for family matters, private and sacred, with no political implications.

But this, in respect to the Catholic church, is a fundamental error. All ancient religions are political. Either in sports, like paganism, or thoroughly and minutely, as in the Jewish law and the Koran, they set out to supply a divine guidance for the government of society, no less than for the private conscience. Their regimen is held to be the sole means of making men sane in this world and happy in the next. If therefore the Catholic church ever became dominant in America, it would without doubt, by virtue of its concrete mission, transform American life and institutions. In the measure of its power and prudence it would abolish religious liberty, the freedom of the press, divorce, and lay education. Whether there is any danger of so surprising a revolution the reader has doubtless better means of judging than

I; but what he perhaps has had no opportunity of discovering is the nature of the constraint which the Catholic church puts upon the life, and especially the religious life, of its members.

Mr. Chapman, for instance, calls it a contradiction that mystical experience, which he finds present in the church, should coexist at all with a system of doctrine and moral government which, as he imagines, intercepts all mystical experience at its source. I see the contradiction between the theory that a thing must be intercepted by certain agencies and the admitted fact that it is not; but apart from infelicities of expression, Mr. Chapman seems to have missed the source of the trouble which undoubtedly exists, and the actual relation between religious experience and religious institutions. The mystical feeling comes first: it can never be intercepted. On occasion of alarming phenomena, like thunder, death, or apparitions, or else welling up without apparent occasion from within, a mysterious emotion seizes the mind automatically. Sceptics may call this experience pathological and say it means nothing, but the person affected always asks what it means. He assumes that it is a revelation of something external or permanent, which it is momentous to take to heart and to report to others. As the senses reveal a material world capable of being mapped out and reacted upon with increasing accuracy by intelligent people, so mystical experience explores the influences under which it arises. It is always taken to reveal a second world, or rather invisible or distant part of this world, knowledge of which may be accumulated and transmitted. It is just so, with a remarkable fidelity to type, that the mystics wish us to take the records of the Psychical Research Society. Just so, too, by experiment and tradition based on the principle that mystical experience is significant, ancient peoples accumulated their elaborate religions.

There is no element in the Catholic system, ancient or modern, that is not the expression of somebody's mystical experience, surprising him either in the creative re-telling of legend, when he sees intuitively what further things *must* have happened, or in spontaneous variations in worship, or in the depths of metaphysical contemplation. What the church has done is to gather these mystical experiences together, in so far as their import is cumulative, eagerly welcoming every new inspiration not incompatible with the old. So grotesquely untrue is the notion that religious institutions must intercept religious experience at its source.

Whence then the cruel rebuffs that some mystics meet with in every church? From this, that the wind bloweth where it listeth, and that religious experiences prompt all sorts of fixed persuasions incompatible with one another. Those of us who live happily enough without revelations may be willing to let these discordant mystics enjoy their several harmonies, like so many rival musical composers, each in his unenvied heaven; but the mystics themselves, being inwardly illuminated, are fiercely intolerant. Any contradiction to the voice of God speaking in their hearts is insufferable to them. What then remains for them to say of the contrary inspirations of others? Only that they are the whisperings of Beelzebub; an opinion which saves the situation for each particular seer, but hardly increases the peace of the mystical household. This brave expedient is far from obsolete. Mr. Chapman regards the spontaneous and sincere insights of Nietzsche as diabolical, because they contradict his own. The insults which the author of "Lead Kindly Light" heaps on the Mohammedans are beyond belief. It is not worldly ecclesiastics that kindle the fires of persecution, but mystics who think they hear the voice of God.

The triumph of the Catholic church, if it were possible, would accordingly not suppress religious experience in America, it would immensely increase and intensify it; but it would tolerate only what it could assimilate. All independent pursuits of truth would be over, the truth in crucial matters being supposed to be known. The sciences, history especially, would have to twist their conclusions to fit the faith, and there would be an end to radical experiments in morals and to the hope of any essential lightening of human burdens. However remotely the church felt that it might be affected by any movement, its fanaticism would be aroused; its intense belief in the supreme importance of its mission would blind it to every other interest; as against its enemies, it would be incapable of so much as the idea of justice, and it would be a placid accomplice to every crime that seemed to make for its ascendency.

This is a frightful prospect enough; failure in all the modern heart is set upon. Yet the world has survived that ordeal once, and would survive it again; and it could still say with Homer: "Endure, my heart; worse things hast thou endured." As Mr. Chapman observed very justly, the Catholic church requires submission, not uniformity. It suppresses obnoxious conclusions when stubbornly maintained; it is remarkably favorable to the play of mind. You are born to an institution, a tradition, a genial and a rich life; you are not stifled in cant or caught in a formula. If you are a good child of the family, romping is allowed. It is not as if everyone were forced to become a Hegelian and to do the same trick every time he opened his mouth. Dante, Chaucer, and Cervantes were entirely docile but entirely different. All a Catholic need do, in letting his genius go, is to say to himself sincerely: "If this is right, let it be used and built into the edifice: if it is wrong, let it pass for an idle fancy. Who am I that I should insist?" This attitude would have saved him from the stake in the middle ages, and nowadays it might save many a man from suicide or the madhouse.

Such humility, if it binds the mind in one sense, liberates it in another. A wit, a satirist, an artist, a man of passionate fancy, finds more sympathy and more feedom in a Catholic atmosphere than in a Protestant one. Nor is the intellect reduced by this reasonable modesty to trivial undertakings. Of course, a man whose inspiration is hostile to tradition will be starved and persecuted; he will have to face death if he is impetuous, and if he is prudent he will be obliged to leave his discoveries unpublished, to be unearthed perhaps by some sympathetic soul in a later generation. But if his inspiration is in harmony with the organic and traditional system about him, itself a product of inspiration, he is buoyed up at once and lifted on the shoulders of a great past; he is supplied with a function and a standard beyond himself. He is not expected to solve every ultimate question offhand. He acquires authority by submitting to it, he can become a master because he has been a pupil. The dignity of an immortal cooperation and unanimity raises him above all pertness and folly. That is the reason why great works of imagination appear only in ages of moral unity, or immediately after, when the grand style, the sure gamut, the voluminous passion of that age are still in the air. Our intellectual liberty is itself a great inheritance, but it deprives us of every other. Each little barbarous mind plays with what pebbles it happens to pick up. No subject is beyond anybody's range, and the temple of opinion is like a shop with the alluring motto: *Nothing over ten cents.*

The Catholic system has many ancient sources, having been developed by the Fathers to unite and console antiquity in its decline, and it is, by the way, far more Greek than Roman in its religious texture. As Mr. Chapman says, "It is the greatest historic residium in the world, the most perfect piece of the past, and it gives us a more accurate measure for judging the past than any other extant institution." But it is also modern, the one complete, stable religion alive under our noses. Without a just understanding of it the present is unintelligible and the future, perhaps, is apt to be miscalculated, for we are still in the era of religions. The mind is deeply perplexed about its origin and without trained courage to face the facts. Yet who takes pains to understand this most human of phenomena?

Mr. Chapman himself is at sea in the subject. He tries occasionally to be fair and then suddenly sees red. It is hard in an external view of inward things to say how much is mere foreign accent and how much positive error. Mr. Chapman is disquieted about the plottings of the clergy in Madison Avenue; the pathos of distance makes them romantic to him. He says that indulgences "condone" sins. He seems to think that the Jesuits are the only leaven in the lump (I mean poison in the well)—as if all the religious orders did not differ in spirit and function from one another and from the secular clergy. He even imagines that people are "drugged" by incense, candles, and "sensationalism." This is as if some aesthetic traveler, on seeing a patriotic crowd waving flags, should take note that a whole nation could be hypnotized by agitated drapery and crude colors. Those who have lost the instinct for expression cannot imagine that those who retain it have anything to express.

The theory that any religion is the work of politicians or sensualists may safely be disregarded. Not even on its political or aesthetic side has any religion such an origin nor does it serve such a purpose. What happens is the exact opposite. Mystical passion and devout fancy intervene spontaneously and powerfully in mundane affairs, and in so doing they at once quicken and confuse science, morals, and politics.

AMERICA'S YOUNG RADICALS

When I was a college professor, I sometimes wondered why there was no socialism among the sophomores. Now that I am not there to welcome it, the thing seems to have come.

I say *to welcome it,* because although I am a high Tory in my sympathies, I recognize that different hearts must be set on different things, and I like young people who have hearts, and who set them on something. It is a great pity if, for lack of self-knowledge or a congenial environment, they set them on the wrong thing, and miss their possible happiness, or miss even the noble martyrdom of knowing why they are unhappy. But they will not have set their hearts on the wrong thing simply because that thing may be indifferent or disagreeable to *me.* My personal feelings have nothing to do with the genuineness of their ideals, or with the worth of their happiness, if they are able to attain it. At most, my experience may make me suspect that these ideals may be unattainable, or that in choosing them these young men, in some cases, may have misunderstood their own nature, and may be pursuing something which, if they got it, would make them very sick. When that is so, a word of warning from an outsider may not be entirely useless.

This essay was published in *The Forum,* May, 1922.

The reason why it is easy to mistake the demands of one's own nature is that human instincts are very complex and confused, and that they mature at different times, or are suppressed or disguised altogether; whereas the fancy is peopled only by the shallow images of such things as we happen to have come upon in our experience. We cannot love, nor warmly imagine, what we have never seen; even when we hate things as we find them (as every fresh soul must in a great measure) our capacity to conceive better things is limited to such hints as actual things have vouchsafed us. We may therefore have no idea at all of what would really satisfy us; even if it were described to us in words, we should not recognize it as our ideal of happiness. It would seem cold, exotic, irrelevant, because nothing of that sort has as yet entered our experience, or lay in the path immediately open before us.

I was accordingly not at all surprised that the life of the ancients, although alone truly human and addressed to a possible happiness, should not appeal to young America. It is too remote, too simple; it presupposes the absence of this vast modern mechanical momentum, this rushing tide of instrumentalities on which young America is borne along so merrily. What surprised me a little was that everybody seemed content to go on swimming and swimming: for even when a man grumbled and worried about his difficulties or mishaps—athletic training, college clubs, family friction, dubious prospects, unrequited love—he yet seemed to be entirely at peace with the general plan of existence as he found it; not at all oppressed by the sense of any surrounding ugliness, vulgarity, vanity, servitude, or emptiness. Was there in these youths, I used to ask myself, so engaging often in their personal ardor, no human soul at all, but rather the soul of some working ant or unquestioning bee, eager to run on its predetermined errands, store its traditional honey, and build its geometrical cell, for the queen of the hive, the future Mrs. Ant or Mrs. Bee, to lay her eggs in? I am far from regarding romantic man as necessarily the best of animals, or a success at all, so far; and I am quite willing he should be superseded, if nature, in America or elsewhere, can evolve a superior species to take his place; but this sudden extinction of human passion seemed a little strange, and I doubted whether perfect happiness in mechanism was as yet possible even for the healthiest, busiest, most athletic, most domestic, and most conventional American. Might not the great American panacea for human wretchedness, Work, be not so much a cure as an anaesthetic?

And now, apparently, the awakening has come, at least to a few, and the sophomores (who are many of them out of college) have discovered the necessity of socialism. I call it socialism for short, although they are not all advocates of socialism in a technical sense, but style themselves liberals, radicals, or (modestly) the *Intelligentsia*. The point is that they all proclaim their disgust at the present state of things in America, they denounce the Constitution of the United States, the churches, the government, the colleges, the press, the theatres, and above all they denounce the spirit that vivifies and unifies all these things, the spirit of Business. Here is disaffection breaking out in which seemed the most unanimous, the most satisfied of nations: here are Americans impatient with America.

Is it simply impatience? Is it the measles, and by the time these sophomores are reverend seniors will it have passed away? Or is it a tragic atavism in individuals, such as must appear sporadically in all ages and nations, an inopportune sport of nature, hatching a bird of paradise in the arctic regions? Even in this case, pathetic as it is, nothing can be done except to wait for the unhappy creatures to come to a fluttering end, for lack of sunshine and appropriate worms. Untoward genius must die in a corner. I am ready to believe that these young radicals are geniuses and birds of paradise, as they evidently feel themselves to be; if so, their plaints ought to make a beautiful elegy; but it would still be a dying song. Or is it possible, on the contrary, that they are prophets of something attainable, boy-scouts with a real army behind them, and a definite future?

I have made a severe effort to discover, as well as I may from a distance, what these rebels want. I see what they are *against*— they are against everything—but what are they *for*? I have not been able to discover it. This may be due to my lack of understanding or to their incapacity to express themselves clearly, for their style is something appalling. But perhaps their scandalous failure in expression, when expression is what they yearn for and demand at all costs, may be a symptom of something deeper: of a radical mistake they have made in the direction of their efforts and aspirations. They think they need more freedom, more room, a chance to be more spontaneous: I suspect that they have had too much freedom, too much empty space, too much practice in being spontaneous when there was nothing in them to bubble out. Their style is a sign of this: it is not merely that they have no mastery of the English language as hitherto spoken, no clear sense of the value of words, and no simplicity; that they are without the vocabulary or the idiom of cultivated people.

That might all be healthy evolution, even if a little disconcerting to us old fogies, who can't keep up with the progress of slang. America has a right to a language of its own, and to the largest share in forming that pigeon-English which is to be the "world-language" of the future. But it is not comparatively only that the style of the young radicals is bad, nor in view of traditional standards: it is bad intrinsically; it is muddy, abstract, cumbrous, contorted, joyless, obscure. If their thoughts were clear, if the images in their minds were definite and fondly cherished, if their principles and allegiances were firm, we should soon learn to read their language and feel it to be pure and limpid, however novel its forms. Dante wrote in a new dialect, provincial and popular; yet how all his words shine like dew on a sunny morning! But Dante had looked long and intently; he had loved silently; he knew what he felt and what he believed. No: it is not more freedom that young America needs in order to be happy: it needs more discipline.

MARGINAL NOTES ON CIVILIZATION IN THE UNITED STATES

What is Civilization? Porcelain bath-tubs, et cetera? Fine art? Free thought? Virtue? Peace? Peace, virtue, and free thought might exist in Arcadia or in the Islands of the Blest, neither of which would be called exactly civilized. Civilized means citified, trained, faithful to some regimen deliberately instituted. Civilization might be taken as a purely descriptive term, like *Kultur*, rather than as a eulogistic one; it might simply indicate the possession of instruments, material and social, for accomplishing all sorts of things, whether those things were worth accomplishing or not. If we insist on taking civilization as a term of praise, we must mean by it something like institutions making for the highest happiness; and what such happiness is could not be defined without plunging into moral philosophy, in which no two persons would agree.

CONTENTS

The list of the thirty American authors of this book, and the three foreigners, makes me tremble. I know a good many of them

Santayana wrote these "Notes" to ideas expressed in *Civilization in the United States, an Inquiry by Thirty Americans,* edited by Harold Stearns, New York, 1922. The comments were published as an essay in *The Dial,* June, 1922.

and some (though this is not the moment to boast of it) have been my pupils. I foresee that I am to hear the plaints of superior and highly critical minds, suffering from maladaptation; and that I shall learn more about their palpitating doubts than about America or about civilization. Nevertheless, as they are a part of America—although they may forget to give America credit for having produced them—I shall be learning something about America after all; and if their strictures upon their country sadden me, I can always comfort myself with a fact which they may be too modest to notice; namely, that civilization can't be at a low ebb where thirty such spirits can be brought together in a jiffy, by merely whistling for them.

PREFACE[1]

"As long ago as the autumn of last year . . . we wished to take advantage of the strategic situation . . . decided . . . by majority vote . . . to be good-natured and . . . urbane. . . . No martyrs, and no one who was merely disgruntled. . . . Slow and careful selection . . . of like-minded men and women . . . in common defense against . . . reaction." Quite as I thought. Indignation at the powers that be is a frequent source of eloquence in Europe; I have not known it before in America on this scale. I shall be all ears.

Page vi. *"There is a sharp dichotomy between preaching and practice; we let not our right hand know what our left hand doeth. . . . The moral code resolves itself into . . . fear of what people will say."* I see the fact which Mr. Stearns points to here, but not as he sees it. The American conscience is not insincere; it is only belated, inapplicable. The sanctities are traditional; sentiment preserves and requires the habits and language of an elder age; it has all the sincerity of instinct. But it does not exactly fit the exigences of public life, which has been transformed and accelerated in a way which conscience can't keep up with, yet is dazzled by and has not the heart to condemn; for it has to keep house, as it were, with an obstreperous younger brother, the conscience of emancipated human nature, with its new set of illusions and its pride in its thundering, pushing life. The Ameri-

---

[1] Written by Harold Stearns.

can intellect is shy and feminine; it paints nature in water-colours; whereas the sharp masculine eye sees the world as a moving-picture—rapid, dramatic, vulgar, to be glanced at and used merely as a sign of what is going to happen next. Mere man in America hardly has an articulate logic in which to express his practical convictions, and I doubt if even this book will supply the want. I won't say that it is itself genteel; that would enrage its revolutionary authors too much; they may have forgotten that Emerson and Thoreau and Brook Farm were revolutionary. But if not genteel and not specifically American, the spirit of these critics is one of offended sensibility. Things shock them; and their compensatory ideals and plans of reform are fetched from abstract reflection or irrelevant enthusiasms. They are far from expressing the manly heart of America, emancipated from the genteel tradition. They seem to be morally underfed, and they are disaffected.

Page vii. *"American civilization is . . . not Anglo-Saxon. . . . Until we begin . . . to cherish the heterogeneous elements which make up our life . . . we shall remain . . . a polyglot boarding-house."* M. Doumic, a French observer, has said that, while the English and Germans are races, the United States, like France, is a *milieu*—what American philosophy calls a "situation." Only in France the memory and discipline of past situations survives in the different classes and parties, in the church, army, government, and literature; whereas in America, apart from a rather pale genteel tradition, only the present situation counts. It is the present task, the present state of business, and present fashion in pleasure that create the hearty unity and universal hum of America—just the unity which these thirty individualists resent, and wish to break up. Why not be patient? Situations change quickly. Why not enjoy moral variety *seriatim* instead of simultaneously? A proof that Americanism is the expression of a present material environment, is that the immigrants at once feel themselves and actually become typical Americans, more instinct with an aggressive Americanism than the natives of Cape Cod or the poor whites in the South. Another consequence is that the whole world is being Americanized by the telephone, the trolley car, the department store, and the advertising press. Americanism, apart from the genteel tradition, is simply modernism—purer in America than elsewhere because less impeded and qualified by survivals of the past, but just as pure in Spanish-Italian Buenos Aires as in Irish Jewish New York. If by cherishing heterogeneous elements, Mr. Stearns means preserving the foreign nationalities in the new environment, I am afraid it is impossible. A leading German whom I questioned on this subject (before the war) assured me that in New York he could not prevail on his children to speak German at home, nor to keep up any German traditions. The contagion and rush of the *milieu* are too strong.

Page vii. *"The mania for petty regulation, the driving, regimentating, and drilling, the secret society and its grotesque regalia, the . . . material organization of our pleasures and gaieties . . . painted devils . . . to frighten us away from the acknowledgment of our spiritual poverty."* It is not so bad as that, not at all Satanic. There ought to have been a chapter in this book on manners and social intercourse. The heartiness of American ways, the feminine gush and the masculine go, the girlishness and high jinks and perpetual joking and obligatory jollity may prove fatiguing sometimes; but children often overdo their sports, which does not prove that they are not spontaneous fundamentally. Social intercourse is essentially play, a kind of perpetual amiable comedy; the relish of it comes of liking our part and feeling we are doing it nicely, and that the others are playing up as they should. The atmosphere of sport, fashion, and wealth is agreeable and intoxicating; certainly it is frivolous, unless some passion is at work beneath, and even then it is all vanity; but in that sense, so is life itself, and a philosopher who is really a philosopher will not quarrel with it on that account. What else than vanity could life possibly be in the end? The point is that it should be spontaneous, innocent, and happily worked out, like a piece of music well-played. Isn't American life distinctly successful in expressing its own spirit?

THE CITY[2]

Page 9–11. *"The highest achievements of our material civilization . . . count as so many symptoms of its spiritual failure . . . escape from the environment . . . exotic architec-*

---

[2] Written by Lewis Mumford.

ture. . . ." It is the common fate of all Christendom that, being based on revolution and barbarian recalcitrancy, it has a divided mind. Its arts cannot proceed ingenuously in a straight line of development, but must struggle on by revivals, adaptations, archaisms, and abortions. I think architecture in America is most promising: the architects are intelligent and well-informed; they are beginning to be prudent; and public taste is very watchful and discriminating. It is not in churches nor in great official edifices that artistic success or originality can be expected, but rather in engineering works, such as sky-scrapers, or else in ordinary private houses, such as in England are called cottages and in America "homes." Shaded streets of detached villas, each in its pocket-handkerchief of land, are distinctively American. With a little more solidity in the materials and a little more repose in the designs, they might be wholly pleasing; and if sometimes they seem chaotic and flimsy, as if they were a row of band-boxes laid on the ground and not houses built on foundations, perhaps they only express the better the shifting population which they shelter. They are the barracks of industrialism, which cannot live in the country, but is spilled out of the towns.

POLITICS[3]

Page 21. [A representative . . . shall be an inhabitant of that state in which he shall be chosen.] *"Find me the worst ass in Congress, and I'll show you a man [whom this regulation has] helped to get there and to stay there. Find me the most shameless scoundrel, and I'll show you another."* I do not think this regulation is at fault; fair representatives might have been chosen by lot like jurymen. The trouble is that salaries, patronage, and the possibility of re-election have turned them into professional politicians. These are just as bad when attached to a national machine as to a local one. Representatives should merely interrupt their private business, during parts of two years when Congress is in session, and then return to the plough, the counter, or the work-shop. At the next election, someone else should be chosen to represent the interests and express the views of his

---

[3] Written by H. L. Mencken.

fellow-citizens. In this way government by the people would not perish from the earth.

Page 23. "*The average congressman . . . is . . . not only incompetent and imbecile, but also incurably dishonest.*" Why exaggerate? "*His knowledge is that of a third-rate country lawyer. . . . His intelligence is that of a country-newspaper editor, or evangelical divine. His standards of honour are those of a country banker. . . .*" Why not? Shouldn't a representative be representative? A reformer, a prophet, an expert, a revolutionary committee sitting in enlightened New York would not be a fair vehicle of popular government. Isn't democracy built on the experience and the conviction that superior people are dangerous, and that the instinct of the common people is a safer guide? But what surprises me more than disbelief in democracy, is this hatred of the country-side. Is agriculture the root of evil? Naturally, the first rays of the sun must strike the east side of New York, but do they never travel beyond?

JOURNALISM[4]

Page 43. "*I fail to find any evidence of widespread disgust with the newspaper as it is.*" Is it worse than the gossip diffused in the old days by barbers and porters? A racy popular paper is like the grave-digger in Hamlet, and I don't blame the people for paying a penny for it.

Pages 45–48. "*All newspapers are controlled by the advertising department. . . . Business is behind government and government is behind business. . . . It is a partnership of swindle.*" Would it be better if government strove to ruin business and business to discredit government? And if government is stable and business prosperous, how is the nation swindled?

Pages 49–50. "*False 'optimism' . . . about the military exploits of Russia's enemies . . . Kolchak and Denekin. . . . 'Lying about Lenin' goes merrily on. . . . The London Labour Herald exposed the trick of Lloyd George . . . the prince of political liars. . . . Mr. Hughes' idiotic . . . attitude.*" This fairly lets the cat out of the bag. Mr. Macy's objection to the American press is

---

[4] Written by John Macy.

not that it is controlled by business or government, but only that this business is capitalistic and this government not a Soviet Republic.

EDUCATION[5]

Page 77. *"Faith . . . in what is called education."* Mr. Lovett calls this the great American superstition, but appears to have great hopes of it himself, if it could only be directed to spreading enlightenment instead of prejudice. With "management of institutions of teaching by the teachers" (which he oddly calls democratic control) "the spoliation of the schools by politicians, the sacrifice of education to propaganda, the tyranny of the hierarchy can be successfully resisted." Page 91. But wouldn't a guild of teachers form an irresponsible hierarchy, imposing their ideas on society when they agreed, and quarrelling among themselves when they did not? If this syndicated enlightenment were simply offered without being imposed, people would go to school only as they go to the dentist, when aching for knowledge; and how often would that be? Freedom—and young America furnishes a proof of this—does not make for enlightenment; it makes for play. A free society would create sports, feasts, religion, poetry, music; its enlightenment would be confined to a few scattered sages, as in antiquity. What brings enlightenment is experience, in the sad sense of this word—the pressure of hard facts and unintelligible troubles, making a man rub his eyes in his waking dream, and put two and two together. Enlightenment is cold water. Education is quite another matter. "The purpose of this college," I heard the Master of Balliol say in 1887, "is to rear servants to the Queen." Education is the transmission of a moral and intellectual tradition, with its religion, manners, sentiments, and loyalties. It is not the instruction given in American schools and colleges that matters much, or that constitutes an American education; what matters is the tradition of alacrity, inquisitiveness, self-trust, spontaneous co-operation and club-spirit; all of which can ripen, in the better minds, into openness to light and fidelity to duty. The test of American education is not whether it

---

[5] Written by Robert Morss Lovett.

produces enlightenment, but whether it produces competence and public well-being. Mr. Lovett does not seem to remember that mankind is a tribe of animals, living by habit and thinking in symbols, and that it can never be anything else. If American education does not transmit such a perfect human discipline as that of a Greek city or of the British upper classes, that is not its fault; it works on a vaster canvas with thinner pigments. But its defect lies in not being thoroughly and deeply enough the very thing which Mr. Lovett condemns it for being—a transmitted life.

SCHOLARSHIP AND CRITICISM[6]

Page 94. *"Spiritual starvation . . . signs of its restless gnawing on the face of almost any American woman beyond the first flush of youth . . . hopeless craving on the face of almost any mature American man."*

Page 98. *"Body but no soul . . . freshness is not there . . . scholars without scholarship . . . churches without religion."* What can be the cause of this dreadful state of things? There are just three causes: Page 101 (1) *"The conception of literature as a moral influence";* (2) *"The . . . conception of literature as the . . . vehicle for a new 'Weltanschauung'";* (3) *"The conception of . . . 'art for art's sake.'"* And there are just three remedies to be applied: Page 105 (1) *"Aesthetic thinking. . . . The haphazard empiricism of English criticism and the faded moralism of our own will serve us no more. . . . We must seek purer and deeper streams. . . . Only in this way can we gain what America lacks, the brain-illumined soul."* (2) *"Knowledge . . . a wider international outlook and a deeper national insight";* (3) *"Training in taste . . . a more complete submission to the imaginative will of the artist."* My own experience does not suggest that Americans are wanting in taste, knowledge, or aesthetic thinking; on the contrary, a great preoccupation and anxiety about these things, a thirst for culture and a desire not to miss or misunderstand anything, seem to be a chief part of their spiritual misery. They are perpetually troubled

---

[6] Written by J. E. Spingarn.

lest they should not fully enjoy the morning sunshine and their delicious oatmeal and cream and cubist painting and the poetry of Miss Amy Lowell; while their love for Botticelli is a tender passion and their preference for Michael Angelo over Raphael is a philosophic conviction. I hardly think that if the aesthetics of Hegel and of Croce were taught in the high schools the facial muscles of the nation would relax and they would burst into passionate song, like Neapolitan minstrels. What I should like somebody to explain is the American voice and language and newspapers; where taste and sensibility are hardened to such a pervasive ugliness (or else affectation) in these familiar things, it is needless to look further for the difficulties which beset the artist, in spite of his high ambitions and enlightenment. The artistic idiom is foreign to him; he cannot be simple, he cannot be unconscious, he has no native, unquestioned, inevitable masters. And it is not easy for native masters to spring up; the moral soil is too thin and shifting, like sand in an hourglass, always on the move; whatever traditions there are, practical men and reformers insist on abandoning; every house is always being pulled down for rebuilding; nothing can take root; nothing can be assumed as a common affection, a common pleasure; no refinement of sense, no pause, no passion, no candour, no enchantment. The thirty authors of this book, for instance, give out that they are the salt of the nation: "We have a vitality and nervous alertness," they say (page 149), "which . . . might cut through the rocks of stupidity. . . . Our cup of life is full to the brim," and I have no reason to doubt it. Yet none of them seems ever to have loved anything; that cup must be filled with a very unpalatable liquid; and this is how they write: "A scheme of undergraduate emphases, grouped and amended as his triumphant progress permitted him to check up on his observations." "A curtailment of potential scientific achievement through the general deficiencies of the cultural environment." "Little of this talent succeeds in effectuating itself." "The fountain-pen with which a great poem is written." "Producing and buying art." "This is not postured for sensational effect." "Essayed to boo it into permanent discard." "Arrived at a degree of theatrical polish sufficient to boast a little playhouse up an ulterior mews." "Sex, save it be presented in terms of a seltzer-siphon, 'Abendstern,' or the *Police Gazette*, spells failure." "Exceptions portend the first signs of the coming dawn." "Formulaic crisis-psychology." "Too little faith in the rationality of the collect to believe that problems can be faced in battalions." "Let a producer break away from the mantel-leaning histrionism and palm-pot investiture, and against him is brought up the curt dismissal of freakishness." "Scarcely time to admire a millionth part . . . before a new and greatly improved universe floats across the horizon and, from every corner news-stand, smilingly bids us enter its portals." Indeed there is scarcely time; and I should be sorry to seem to break away with the curt dismissal of freakishness, but I can't help agreeing with what I have marked on another page, that "our ways of expression are very wasteful" and that "when these rebels really begin to think, the confusion is increased."

SCHOOL AND COLLEGE LIFE[7]

Page 109. *"American . . . cities are only less identical than the trains that ply between them."* Yes; when I went to California I discovered that West Newton, Mass., extends to the Pacific. Page 112. *"Americans are . . . uniformly charming."* In intention they are; they come forward smiling, "happy to meet you," and apparently confident that the happiness will be mutual; they beam as if sure to charm; but are they uniformly charming in fact? Charm seems to rest on something more than conventional kindness and effusiveness, on subtle gifts which are not voluntary. Page 113. *"If our convictions . . . sprang from real knowledge of ourselves and of our capacities, we should relish egoists, disinterested critics, intellectuals, artists, and irreverent humorists."* Each such person would relish himself, even if they did not relish one another. But Americans are diffident, often feigning an assurance which they are far from feeling, and not able heartily to snap their fingers at public opinion. The instinct and the ideal of uniformity are very profound in them; if they are compelled to be rebels, they become propagandists, like the authors of this book, and if they cannot conform to the majority they are not happy until they make the majority conform to them. Why this passion? Page 114. The teacher is *"a harassed young*

---

[7] Written by Clarence Britten.

*woman . . . who has to answer, or silence, the questions of from
a score to three score mouths. So begins that long throttling of
curiosity which later on will baffle the college instructor.*" This is
an effect of being taught in classes; we listen to the droning
recitation or lecture as to the patter of rain. I believe in schools,
especially in boarding-schools and colleges, because I think they
are good for the character, and a relief to the family and from the
family; but they are bad for the intellect. A spark, no doubt, will
fly occasionally from the teacher and kindle some thought or
interest in the pupil; but he must depend for stimulus on what he
can pick up from books and from casual contacts. Fortunately the
school or college gives him intellectual leisure and space, and
allows him to brood; so that if there is intellect enough in him to
be worth asserting, it can assert itself. Page 116. "*The American
undergraduate is representative of the American temper at its
best. . . . As he thinks and feels, all America would think and
feel if it dared and could.*" Yes; and what an immense improvement it would be! The undergraduate is not devoted to making
money; he is not subject to women; he does, except when the
pressure or fear of the outer world constrains him, only what he
finds worth doing for its own sake. I wish reformers, instead of
trying to make the colleges more useful and professional, would
try to make the world more like the colleges. The things that the
world might find worth doing for their own sake would perhaps
be nobler than those that appeal to the undergraduate, though I
am far from confident of that; but in any case, means would no
longer be pursued as ends. The world would then shine with
what is called honour, which is allegiance to what one knows one
loves.

SCIENCE[8]

Page 151. "*In art . . . mediocrity is worthless and incapable of
giving inspiration to genius. But in science . . . every bit of
sound work . . . counts.*" It counts in art also, when art is alive.
In a thoroughly humanized society everything—clothes, speech,
manners, government—is a work of art, being so done as to be a
pleasure and a stimulus in itself. There seems to be an impression

---

[8] Written by Robert H. Lowie.

in America that art is fed on the history of art, and is what is
found in museums. But museums are mausoleums, only dead art
is there, and only ghosts of artists flit about them. The priggish
notion that an artist is a person undertaking to produce immortal
works suffices to show that art has become a foreign thing, an
hors-d'oeuvre, and that it is probably doomed to affectation and
sterility. Page 155. *"American science . . . is . . . a hot-house
growth."* I am surprised to hear this, as I supposed that astronomy, chemistry, natural history, and medicine were nowhere
more at home. That science may have practical applications, or
even may be pursued in view of them, does not seem to me to
militate against its scientific purity, nor against a pure enthusiasm
for knowledge. It is again as in art; the thrill, the vision, the
happy invention come to the faithful workman as a free gift, in
the midst of his labour.

THE LITERARY LIFE[9]

Page 180. *"The chronic state of our literature is that of a
youthful promise which is never redeemed."* The fate of the
Harvard poets in my time—Sanborn, McCulloch, Stickney,
Lodge, Savage, Moody—was a tragic instance of this. If death
had not cut them all off prematurely, would they have fulfilled
their promise? I think that Moody, who actually accomplished
most, would have succeeded notably, in that as a dramatist or as
a poet with a mission, he would have secured general attention
and respect; but even so, it might have been at the expense of his
early poetic colour and disinterested passion for beauty. Stickney, who was the one I knew best, could never, I am sure, have
prospered in the American air. Although he was a Harvard man,
he had been well taught privately first, then afterwards for many
years studied in Paris. When he returned to Harvard to teach
Greek, he was heroically determined to take the thing seriously,
and to share enthusiastically the life of his country; but the
instrument was far too delicate and sensitive for the work; his
imaginative (yet exact) learning, his spiritual ardour, his remote
allegiances (as for instance to Indian philosophy) could not have
survived the terrible inertia and the more terrible momentum of

---

[9] Written by Van Wyck Brooks.

his new environment. Not that America does not afford material opportunities and even stimulus for the intellectual life, provided it is not merely retrospective or poetical; a man like William James, whose plough could cut into rough new ground, left an indelible furrow; but he had a doctor's healthy attitude towards human ills, his Pragmatism was a sort of diagnosis of America, and even he would have found it uphill work to cultivate beauty of form, to maintain ultimate insights, or to live in familiar friendship with the Greeks and the Indians. I managed it after a fashion myself, because I was conscious of being a foreigner with my essential breathing tubes to other regions; nor did I really belong to the irritable genius; I had perhaps more natural stamina, less fineness, more unconcern, and the spirit of mockery, in the last resort, to protect me.

MUSIC[10]

Page 210. *"The American composer . . . works more or less in a vacuum. He is out of things and he knows it."* Why should he mind that? Music is a world above the worlds, and the ladder into it can be planted anywhere. I suspect the difficulty lies in a divided allegiance: the musician will not live on music alone, he is no true musician. Snobbery, the anxiety to succeed, and a sort of cowardly social instinct stand between the artist and his work. It is because he wants "to be in things" that he fails, and deserves to fail.

ECONOMIC OPINION[11]

Page 255. *"The idea that knowledge . . . is essential to the right to an opinion . . . is little understood here."* Because opinions are regarded as expressing people and not things. This is a consequence of modern philosophy, or the principle of it. All opinions are free and equal if, as modern philosophy maintains, they have no objects and are essentially opinions about nothing; the truth can then only be a harmony or a compromise established among these opinions. You shake the ballots in a hat, and pull out salvation.

---

[10] Written by Deems Taylor.
[11] Written by Walter H. Hamilton.

RADICALISM[12]

Page 277. "*Radicalism arises neither from a . . . desire for more material goods, nor from . . . a particular formula. . . . It arises from a desire to be free, to achieve dignity and independence. . . . To be poor . . . is less annoying than to be moderately well paid while the man who fixes one's wages rides in a Rolls-Royce. . . . You may challenge [the workman] to prove that any other system would work better. . . . Reasoning will affect him little. He . . . wants . . . power.*" If envy is the only motive making for a revolution, the revolution will not come except by force of a great delusion; because if the people *knew* that it would bring them no satisfaction but the satisfaction of envy, they would not want it. As to power, it is only the leaders who would have it, and would "Ride in a Rolls-Royce" in the people's service; and accordingly it is only they who would profit by the revolution, since the satisfaction of envy is no benefit, but a new bitterness, like breaking another child's toys; you wanted those fine things for yourselves and you have made them impossible for anybody. It is very characteristic of "radicalism" to boast in this way that it is unreasonable and mean and to ask you threateningly what you will do about it. For my own part, I can do nothing, except be very sorry for the radicals and for the people they would feed on the satisfaction of envy.

THE SMALL TOWN[13]

Page 296. "*There obviously cannot be among such a naturally healthy people a supercilious contempt for sentiment. . . . We may listen to the band concert on a Saturday night in the Court House Square with a studied indifference. . . . But deep down in our hearts is a feeling of invincible pride.*" Here at last is a note of affection; also some rays of humor. Perhaps the extreme complacency about America that is characteristic of the majority, and the profound discomfort and shamefacedness of the minority, when it becomes critical, have a common root in the habit of thinking in terms of comparison, of perpetual competition; either a thing must be the biggest and best in the world, or you must

[12] Written by George Soule.
[13] Written by Louis Raymond Reid.

blush for it. But only ways and means are good comparatively
and on a single scale of values. Anything good intrinsically,
anything loved for its own sake, is its own standard, and
sufficient as it is. The habit of always comparing it with something else is impertinent and shallow. It betrays a mind that
possesses nothing, loves nothing, and is nothing.

THE FAMILY[14]

Pages 334–336. *"The asylums are . . . crowded. . . . The
groundwork for fatal ruptures . . . is laid . . . in the
home. . . . Parents . . . never entertain a modest doubt as to
whether they might be the best of all possible company for their
children. . . . They need themselves to understand and practise
the art of happiness."* The prevalence of insanity, of "breaking
down," and of "nervous depression" is one of the most significant
things in America. It goes with overwork, with not having a
religion or "getting religion" (which is an incident to not having
one), with absence of pleasures, forced optimism, routine, essential solitude. An intense family life would prevent all these miser-
ies, but it would take away personal liberty. The modern family
is only the egg-shell from which you are hatched; there you have
your bed, clothes, meals, and relations; your life is what occupies
you when you are out. But as you foregather only with chicks of
your own age, who are as destitute as yourself, you remain
without the moral necessaries. The test of a good school or
college is its capacity to supply them. It is the only remaining
spiritual home.

ADVERTISING[15]

Page 395. *"Outdoor advertising . . . should be removed from
sight with all possible haste."* A truly radical view. It is not to the
eye only that America would be entirely transformed if a severe
paternal government abolished advertising. The key of the whole
symphony would be lowered, the soft pedal put on. Imagine the
change in speed, if you were reduced to consulting your inner

---

[14] Written by Katharine Anthony.
[15] Written by J. Thorne Smith.

man before buying anything or going anywhere, and to discovering first whether you really wanted anything, and what it was! And imagine, when your inner need had become clear and peremptory all of itself, having to inquire of some shy official, or of some wise stranger, whether just the suit of clothes, or the play or the tour which your soul dreamt of could possibly be brought anywhere into the realm of fact, or must remain a dream for ever! It would not be often that geography or theatrical managers or tailors would have providentially anticipated your wishes, or would consent to realize them; so that your wants would soon be marvellously reduced and your soul chastened. But I suppose the idea of these radical reformers is that this very paternal government, in abolishing advertising, would supply you with such clothes and such dramas and such holiday excursions as you *ought* to want, and when you *ought* to want them. It would be a reversion to antiquity, to the pious peace and leisure of the most remote province in the most backward country. Personally I should have no objection; but is this the revolutionary ideal of "civilization in America"?

BUSINESS[16]

Pages 413–414. "*Business is . . . blind . . . with extravagant reflex powers of accommodation and extension and almost no faculty of original imagination. . . . It has brought about a marvellous economy of human effort. At the same time . . . it wastes the living machine in recurring periods of frightful and unnecessary idleness. . . . It wastes the spirit . . . in the effort to create new and extravagant wants.*" Admirable summary; inventions and organization which ought to have increased leisure, by producing the necessaries with little labour, have only increased the population, degraded labour, and diffused luxury.

SPORT AND PLAY[17]

Page 458. "*Its true . . . function is the cultivation of bodily vigour, with a view to longevity.*" Unless this is ironical—and I

---

[16] Written by Garet Garrett.
[17] Written by Ring W. Lardner.

am sometimes in doubt how to interpret the style of these authors—it is an astonishingly illiberal thing to say. What is the use of longevity? If you said that the purpose of sport was health, that would come nearer the truth, because health at least suggests a *good* life, and is a part of what makes life worth having as it runs, which the length of life is not. The Greeks would have said that the purposes of gymnastics were beauty and military fitness; this too would be a more acceptable thing to say, since beauty and fitness for war and for victory contribute, like health, to the zest and dignity of existence, while existence lasts. But essentially sport has no purpose at all; it is an end in itself, a part of that free fruition of life which is the purpose of other things, when they are good for anything, and which, when present, can make a long life better than a short one. Its possible uses are incidental, like those of the fine arts, religion, or friendship. Not to see this is to be a barbarian.

HUMOUR[18]

Pages 463–466. *"Belief in American humour is a superstition. . . . The prolongation of a single posture of the mind is intolerable. . . . If by a happy stroke of fancy a cow in the dining-room is made pleasing to the mind . . . with the presentation of nine cows in nine dining-rooms it has changed to pain."* I agree that a perpetual search for the incongruous, even if it keeps us laughing mechanically, is empty and vulgar and disgusting in the end. It is a perpetual punning in images. And yet I feel that there is a genuine spirit of humour abroad in America, and that it is one of the best things there. The constant sense of the incongruous, even if artificially stimulated and found only in trivial things, is an admission that existence is absurd; it is therefore a liberation of the spirit over against this absurd world; it is a laughing liberation, because the spirit is glad to be free; and yet it is not a scornful nor bitter liberation, because a world that lets us laugh at it and be free is after all a friendly world. We have no need to bear that serious grudge against it which we should be justified in bearing if it fooled us altogether, and tortured us by its absurdities instead of amusing us and making us spiritually free.

---

[18] Written by Frank M. Colby.

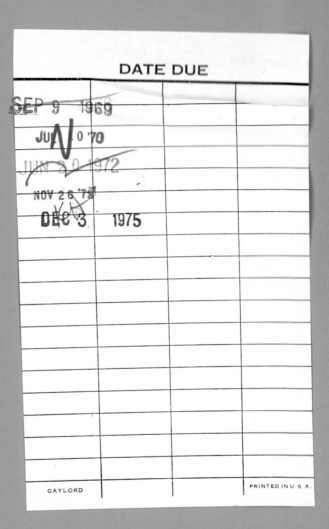

DATE DUE

SEP 9 1969			
JUN 0 70			
JUN 0 1972			
NOV 26 '73			
DEC 3 1975			
GAYLORD			PRINTED IN U.S.A.